CU00665913

VERSAILLES

VERSA

Text by
VALÉRIE BAJOU

Translated by
ANTONY SHUGAAR

AILLES

ABRAMS,
NEW YORK

CHÂTEAU
DE VERSAILLES

PREFACE

The millions of visitors who come to Versailles every year are certainly fascinated by the Hall of Mirrors, the wealth and splendor of a monarchy. At the center of the palace, the chamber of Louis XIV commands "the city and the world" [*urbi et orbi*], while the apartments, the galleries, the rooms of the museum, and the North and South wings follow the story with emotion, as the scenes suggest celebrations, politics, intrigues, but also grief, wars, and peace treaties.

Born from Louis XIV's desire to move away from Paris, the daydreams of celebrations in the first castle, the story of Versailles calls up many feelings. But the departure of the royal family on October 6, 1789, a century after the establishment of the Court, began a period of grieving that did not end until Louis-Philippe's reinvention of Versailles. The opening of the museum in 1837 elevated the king from citizen to savior, even a descendant of Louis XIV.

Éditions de La Martinière has selected recent photographs to give a faithful representation of a visit to the palace today. Thus, a new Versailles, monarchical and republican, is shown, where public lives and private lives are merged. The visitor is surrounded by galleries and remarkable works, described in detail in this book. Then, moving toward the Trianon, ornaments of charming vivacity create a magical setting, while the disciplined lines of the parterres are softened by hedges. But nothing is as magnificent as the park, the Orangerie, the groves inhabited by the gods of an abandoned Olympus, which were photographed throughout the year.

BÉATRIX SAULE Director of the National Museum of the Palace of Versailles and the Trianon

1
Pierre Patel (1605–1676)
Panoramic View of the Palace and the Gardens of Versailles, ca. 1668
Oil on canvas, 115 × 161 cm

THE HISTORY OF VERSAILLES

Versailles is a mirage, a sumptuous and theatrical enchantment. It is also a manifestation of glory and power imposed to a great extent by art, luxury, and magnificence. The mythical dimension of the place is all the more impressive when you learn that before it was a palace, it was a swath of untilled countryside, dotted with ponds and swamps.

Versailles was originally a large expanse of land located near a small town with a church and a few windmills. Surrounded by wilderness, the estate's forests and fields made a perfect hunting ground. Albert de Gondi brought King Henry III and his cousin, Henry of Navarre, the future King Henry IV, there to hunt. Throughout his reign, the latter king continued to hunt there, accompanied by the young Dauphin. In 1622 and 1623, Louis XIII purchased acreage from the de Gondi family, eventually acquiring the entire lot. The French kings were attracted by the abundance of game on the land as well as its proximity to the royal palace in Saint-Germain-en-Laye, but nothing hinted at the greatness that was to come.

CHÂTEAU OF THE FIELDS AND CHÂTEAU OF PAPER

In 1623 Louis XIII ordered the construction of a lodge at the top of a rise to provide convenient housing for his hunting trips. A central block framed by two narrow wings, the brick-and-stone building topped by a pitched slate roof was quite ordinary; the Marshal de Bassompierre called it simply the "country house"—literally, *château des champs*, or château of the fields. Before long, however, the architect Philibert Le Roy transformed this hunting

lodge into a more sumptuous residence situated at the heart of an estate that steadily grew in size. The court, which usually followed the king from one royal house to another in the Île-de-France and the Loire Valley, was not allowed to go there; neither was the royal family.

King Louis XIV was only four years old when he ascended the throne following the death of King Louis XIII in 1643. During a period known as the Regency, the queen consort, Anne of Austria, governed as regent with Cardinal Mazarin in the young king's stead. But an aristocratic uprising, known as the Fronde (1648–1653), forced young Louis XIV to flee Paris and take refuge in the Château de Saint-Germain.

During the early years of his reign, King Louis XIV rarely traveled to Versailles. But following his marriage and the death of the cardinal-minister, and with the memory of the Fronde still all too vivid, the king was encouraged to spend time away from Paris and began staying at Versailles frequently. He soon set about beautifying and enlarging the palace, despite other major construction projects occuring simultaneously—the completion of the Louvre (begun during the reign of Charles V) and of the Palais des Tuileries and the Château de Vincennes.

It was no accident that the work at Versailles began in 1661, immediately following a lavish party given by Nicolas Fouquet, Superintendent of Finance, in honor of the king on August 17th of that year in his château at Vaux-le-Vicomte. To show off such opulence turned out to be a faux pas of the worst sort and resulted in the minister's fall from grace. Wary of Fouquet's power and influence, Louis XIV had him thrown into prison, then commandeered the skills of the team that had designed Fouquet's magnificent château—the architect Louis Le Vau, the landscape designer André Le Nôtre, and the painter Charles Le Brun—to carry out his plans for Versailles.

Before long, the festivities that took place at the château of Versailles, and especially in its gardens, revealed the young king's infatuation with the property. Spectators were astonished by the music, the theater, and the ballets of the *Plaisirs de l'île enchantée* (*Pleasures of the Enchanted Island*) produced in 1664 for Louise de La Vallière and those of the *Grand Divertissement Royal* in 1668 to celebrate France's victory over Spain in the War of Devolution. In order to preserve the memory of the events, the fabulist Jean de La Fontaine published two stories in verse, *Les amours de Psyché et Cupidon* (*The Loves of Cupid and Psyche*) and *La grotte de Versailles* (*The Grotto of Versailles*).

Some critics turned up their noses at the overly traditional and, perhaps, even archaic style of the architecture of Louis XIV's beloved palace. To some of his contemporaries, the architecture possessed neither style nor grandeur; the Duke of Saint-Simon considered it to be nothing more than a "paper castle." All the same, Versailles would become the heart of the French government, where the whole country would converge for more than a century.

CONSTRUCTION GAMES

During the reign of Louis XIV, no fewer than three architects worked in succession to both enhance the splendor of the royal residence and to improve the conveniences of everyday life. Beginning in 1668, Louis Le Vau undertook the construction of the "new castle," whose western facade was comprised of two pavilions separated by a terrace. This construction doubled the size of the old castle, both enlarging and safeguarding the original residence. Using a method that came to be known as Le Vau's envelope solution, the expansion was achieved by enveloping the old château with a facade on three sides that transformed the gaps between the old and new buildings into interior courtyards. The Italian-style palace was topped by a flat roof that combined the rigor of straight lines and respect for proportion and symmetry with unrivaled splendor. The facades were punctuated by frontispieces topped by monumental statues.

In 1678, Jules Hardouin-Mansart took charge of the construction and had even more ambitious plans. In fact, the king had just announced his decision to make Versailles his principal residence. This preference for Versailles over the Louvre was eminently political: Louis XIV hoped to continue the process started by his father—to centralize government around an absolute monarch. By distancing himself from Paris

2
Charles Le Brun (1619–1690)
Portrait of Louis XIV, 1661–1662
Oil on canvas, 67 × 57 cm

3
Jean–Baptiste Martin (1658 or 1659–1735)
View of the Courts of the Palace of Versailles and the Stables, 1688
Oil on canvas, 260 × 184 cm

and forcing the nobility to travel to Versailles, potential rivals were less likely to accrue regional power. Also, by making such an opulent residence the capitol of the kingdom and the seat of government, it highlighted the prestige of France.

At the very same time that the monarch was undertaking foreign wars of conquest, the palace was a sprawling construction site supervised by Jean-Baptiste Colbert, Superintendent of Finance and of Buildings, Arts, and Manufacturing, who was soon promoted to the rank of Controller-General. The various rounds of costly construction and embellishment (1661, 1668, 1678, and 1683) were accompanied by military campaigns that also drained the public coffers—such as the particularly costly War of the League of Augsburg (1688–1697) and the even more expensive War of the Spanish Succession (1701–1714).

Versailles, now the seat of the government, soon grew to the size of a vast city, all conceived around the royal personage. The west-facing terrace (between the apartments of the king and the queen) was quickly replaced by a long gallery that would one day be known as the Hall of Mirrors. And it became necessary to construct new buildings to house the royal family and the court, who moved in on May 6, 1682. On either side of the central structure, two wings were constructed, extending the palace to the south and north and providing housing for the courtiers and the chief ministers. In addition to the wings, which housed the services of the state, the ministries, and, in particular, the Chancellery and the Superintendence of Buildings, the following structures were completed: the Grand Commune building used to house the royal kitchens and staff that served the king's table; the Small Stable for draft horses and carriages; the Grand Stable for riding horses; a tennis court; and a kennel. Moreover, the palace's interior decoration was to be sumptuous. The Ambassadors' Staircase, built in 1672 to serve the apartment of the king, exemplifies the grand scope of the project to improve the palace's interior.

Louis XIV and his successors never tired of building, and this was not limited to the château itself. For example, Louis XV ordered the construction of the Ministry of War and Ministry of Foreign Affairs in the town of Versailles. New work ensued following the death of Louis XIV's wife, Maria Theresa, in 1683. However, Jean-Baptiste Colbert died prior to the completion of the Hall of Mirrors, then known as the Grand Gallery, so he never saw the full décor of the royal apartments he had designed, with their painted ceilings, walls covered with polychrome marble, and rich brocade curtains.

The last construction project of the reign of Louis XIV was the chapel, begun by Jules Hardouin-Mansart and completed by his brother-in-law, Robert de Cotte, in 1710. By that point, the palace's atmosphere was marked by mourning following the death of the Grand Dauphin in 1711, and then the deaths of the Duke and Duchess of Burgundy in 1712.

THE INCEPTION OF PRIVACY

On the exterior, the palace a visitor sees today is not very different from the palace that Louis XIV knew, but the interior is quite another matter. Louis XV preserved, completed, and renovated the work of his grandfather and then, in the end, destroyed as much as he built. The château lost the Ambassadors' Staircase, but gained the Royal Opera.

As for the bedroom built by Louis XIV in 1701, his successor transformed it into the *Chambre de Parade*, where the ceremonial bed was located. The highly elaborate, traditional court etiquette was preserved—where aristocrats would vie for the king's favor, which was demonstrated by being allowed to participate in his rising (*Lever*) and retiring (*Coucher*) ceremonies—while the king did his best to ensure his own comfort. In 1738, the king created a more modern bedchamber in a former billiards room, but still returned to the bed in the *Chambre de Parade* for the traditional *Lever* begun by his grandfather. By that time, most activities took place in the king's private apartment—a space that suggests a more intimate, personal side of Versailles.

Was Louis XV bored at Versailles? Perhaps—it would explain why he fled the court and the rigors of its etiquette to take refuge under the roof of the Grand Trianon, then ordered the construction of the Petit Trianon and took greater interest in his botanical garden. The royal infatuation with the Trianon persisted throughout the reign of Louis XVI, with the development of the Petit Trianon for Marie Antoinette and the creation of a full-fledged village, the Queen's Hamlet.

THE GRAND PLAN

Encouraged by two architects, Ange-Jacques Gabriel and Jean-François Blondel, Louis XV had the idea to conceal the old château behind a number of stone buildings that would match the facades facing the gardens. He ordered the reconstruction of one of the wings overlooking the royal court and the pavilion in this classical style. Was this an attempt to create stylistic unity or simply an effort to insure the privacy of the apartments overlooking the Marble Court? Whichever it was, the project,

4
Étienne Allegrain (1644–1736)
View of the Palace and the Orangerie of Versailles, ca. 1690–1700
Oil on canvas, 115 × 165 cm

begun by Louis XV and continued by Louis XVI, was never completed.

FROM THE FRENCH REVOLUTION TO THE HISTORICAL GALLERIES

The events that led up to the French Revolution began in Versailles with the opening of the Estates General, an assembly formed to represent the church, the common people, and the nobility, in the courtyard of the *Hôtel des Menus Plaisirs* on May 5, 1789. On October 6th, a few months after the storming of the Bastille, Louis XVI, Marie Antoinette, and their children were forced to leave the palace and move to Paris. In the collective imagination, as well as in historical memory, that day marked a concrete barrier between two worlds: No ruler ever again dared live in the palace, ending forever its life as a royal residence, seat of the monarchy, and center of the government.

After the king's execution on January 21, 1793, the Convention, an assembly that governed France from 1792 to 1795, confiscated the palace, making it a property of the French Republic. Although the palace at Versailles was not completely destroyed during the French Revolution, the symbols of the French monarchy—the royal crown, the double L, and the fleurs-de-lis—were zealously effaced. The collections of paintings and sculpture, the objets d'art and books, some of the furniture, and even the animals in the menagerie were parceled out to various Parisian institutions. Because the new republic needed hard cash, the collection of objects and pieces of furniture was sold through public sales and scattered to many new owners, with the most important items remaining in France. Maintenance of the palace's gardens was lackadaisical at best, and dilapidated huts sprang up on the grounds. The gardens, which were open to the public, were used alternatively as vegetable gardens, orchards, and nurseries. In addition, the town of Versailles lost its administrative role and trade declined.

The onetime symbol of a flawed and fallen monarchy, Versailles eventually became a public space for exhibiting the arts and diffusing knowledge. A number of institutions were established there: a natural history collection, a class for sketching and drawing from life, a school of music, and most important, the special museum of the French École des

Beaux-Arts established in March 1797, where contemporary artworks were exhibited beneath ceiling panels painted by Charles Le Brun. Reconciling the palace's royal architectural style with the republic's demand for a museum, Versailles went on to play a role in establishing France's national identity, becoming a symbol of France rather than a particular leader or government; this symbol was carried on by each successive regime. During the First Empire, however, the museum began to decline, and Napoleon's plans to house Marie Louise in the former apartment of the queen never came to fruition, despite the plans drawn up by the architect Jacques Gondoin.

VERSAILLES, OLD AND NEW

Louis Philippe, King of France from 1830 to 1848, a period of liberal constitutional monarchy known as the July Monarchy, told the world that he had rescued Versailles from ruin. This political maneuver, relayed efficiently by the press, formed part of a body of propaganda that did not acknowledge the many reconstruction projects that had been undertaken before his reign.

Although the château was no longer used as a royal residence during the Restoration, it was never completely abandoned. The reconstruction began with inserting the royal emblems throughout the palace, and Louis XVIII decorated several rooms during his rule from 1814 to 1824.

Louis Philippe did, however, shape the role of the palace in an innovative way. With an acute awareness of history enlivened by the French Revolution and sensitized by the Romantic movement, Louis Philippe decided to make Versailles into a museum consecrated "to all the glories of France." From one end to the other, the king arranged the palace's art into important groupings: the Gallery of Battles; the Hall of the Estates General; the Hall of 1792; the Hall of the Sacred, which corresponded to the Hall of 1830; and finally, the Halls of the

Crusades and the Halls of Africa, both left unfinished after the fall of the July Monarchy. Louis Philippe personally supervised these projects and issued weekly directives to the palace architect, Frédéric Nepveu.

The inauguration of the Historical Galleries took place on June 10, 1837, as part of the festivities honoring the wedding of Ferdinand-Philippe d'Orléans and Helene of Mecklenburg-Schwerin; it was an occasion for a spectacle that was at once monarchic and popular, where representatives of an older French society mingled with the leading figures of the new France. Among the guests were artists who had received royal commissions, but Victor Hugo, Charles Augustin Sainte-Beuve, Alexandre Dumas, *père*, Jules Michelet, Alfred de Vigny, and Alfred de Musset also attended, all eager to be part of the show. A symbolic high point of the tour took place at the heart of the château in the grand chamber of the king where the venerated monarchic tradition of the *Chambre de Parade*, the *apartment d'étiquette*, displayed the embarrassing heritage of the Bourbon dynasty for all to see. Louis Philippe's efforts allowed the palace's history to be placed in an educational framework that used the past to understand the present, an approach underscored by Victor Hugo: "What Louis Philippe did at Versailles was a good thing [...] He established the present in the midst of the past, 1789 with respect to 1688, the emperor in the residence of the king, Napoleon in the presence of Louis XIV; in a word, what he did was to give this magnificent book we call the history of France, the magnificent binding that we call Versailles."*

Louis Philippe was forced to abdicate in 1848. Yet despite the succession of revolutions that continued to plague France, the transitions from one regime to the next were smooth. On

---

* Victor Hugo, *Feuilles paginées III*, in *Œuvres complètes*, chronological edition published under the supervision of Jean Massin, Paris, Le Club Français du Livre, 1967–1970, volume V, p. 1015–16.

5
Hyacinthe Rigaud (1659–1743)
Portrait of Louis XV, 1730

Oil on canvas, 276.5 × 186 cm, Hall of the King's Guards

6
Antoine-François Callet (1741–1823)
Portrait of Louis XVI, 1789

Oil on canvas, 278 × 196 cm, Apollo Drawing Room

7
Horace Vernet (1789–1863)
King Louis-Philippe and His Sons in Front of the Palace of Versailles, 1846
Oil on canvas, 367 × 394 cm, Drawing Room of 1847, Questel Staircase

February 25, 1848, the new minister for foreign affairs for the Second Republic, Alphonse de Lamartine, announced to the mayor of Versailles that, "the provisional government wishes to inform you that it takes the artistic monument of Versailles under its protection." An artistic monument: Is that what Versailles had become? It is true that orders and commissions became less frequent, and during the Second Empire, the curator Eudore Soulié created only two new rooms in the north wing. However, the palace remained the setting for sumptuous fetes held to honor visiting foreign rulers such as Queen Victoria, when she came to Paris to tour the 1855 Exposition Universelle, and Prince Francisco de Asís de Borbón, Duke of Cádiz and husband of Queen Isabella II of Spain.

When the Franco-Prussian War of 1870 broke out, the museum had virtually been forgotten. Still, Versailles remained a powerful political symbol. That is why Wilhelm I, King of Prussia, at the insistence of his chancellor, Otto von Bismarck, had himself proclaimed emperor of Germany on January 18, 1871, in the Hall of Mirrors following France's defeat. The palace was again occupied when the government of Adolphe Thiers—fleeing the chaos of the Paris Commune, a socialist group that briefly ruled France after the Franco-Prussian War—was evacuated to Versailles in March 1871. The French parliament only returned to Paris in 1879. Every seven years until 1953, the two chambers of the French parliament met in joint session to elect the president of the French Republic in the *Salle du Congrès* (Congress Room) built in the south wing in 1875.

THE REVIVAL OF VERSAILLES

Credit for the revival of Versailles is due to the curator Pierre de Nolhac, a scholar of Petrarch and of the Pléiade (a group of sixteenth-century French Renaissance poets), who originally worked under Charles Gosselin. On September 9, 1889, not long before Nolhac succeeded Gosselin as curator in 1892, Versailles became a national museum, but it was not until 1906 that it was classified as a historic monument. For thirty years, Pierre de Nolhac's work focused on two complementary principles: to restore the original sheen and glow of the royal residence and to reorganize the halls of national history. The fact that his choices are still followed today is an indication of the mythical status he still enjoys among the curators.

The renovation was brutal and irrevocable: Nolhac, a ruthless iconoclast when it came to the efforts of Louis Philippe, eliminated many of the king's creations in order to restore the apartments of the Ancien Régime. "In less than a year," Nolhac explains in his book, *La Résurrection de Versailles, souvenirs d'un conservateur* (*The Resurrection of Versailles: Memories of a Curator*), "the iconographic creations of Louis Philippe had been destroyed, his decorative undertakings rendered unusable, and I could be certain that, in the sections that had just been overhauled, nothing could ever be reconstructed of that past [...] That is the goal that, as everyone knows, organizers of revolutions must expect from the very first day." Aided by the support of the Society of the Friends of Versailles (founded in 1909), he preserved only the Halls of the Battles and the Hall of 1830, the Halls of the Empire, the Halls of the Crusades, and the Halls of Africa. Most important, he radically rethought the presentation of the collections and decided that, from that point forward, no art would be hung that was not painted by a contemporary of the events depicted. The historical paintings of the nineteenth century were removed and replaced by paintings of current events and reportage. Charles Mauricheau-Beaupré, appointed curator in 1945, and after him, Gérald van der Kemp, who became curator in 1953, extended this principle of contemporary depiction, which had incorrectly been taken as a standard of authenticity, to the entire château.

Nolhac attracted a political, literary, and artistic elite to Versailles that ensured the success of the château. He welcomed such prominent personalities as Alphonse Daudet, Anatole France, Jules Massenet, Robert de Montesquiou, Marcel Proust, and Pierre Puvis de Chavannes, who delivered a lecture on Le Brun; he was also asked to welcome the Empress Eugénie, Prince Henri, Duke of Aumale, Nicholas II in 1896, and Edward VII in 1903.

In response to the start of World War I, the château closed its doors in August 1914, but most of the collections remained in place until the museum again opened to the public in April 1915. In the spring of 1918, the artwork was packed in crates and stored under the shelter of the northern stone gallery. Seen by some as revenge for the 1871 Treaty of Versailles that ended the Franco-Prussian War, the Treaty of Versailles that ended World War I was signed on June 28, 1919, in the Hall of Mirrors, while the negotiations for peace in Europe were carried out with the Interallied Commission at the Trianon Palace.

With the support of a number of government acts providing the framework for the program, the work first begun by Pierre de Nolhac was accelerated after World War II. Among the restoration projects undertaken were those of the queen's bedroom, the king's bedroom, the Royal Opera, and the renovation of the Grand Trianon. For a number of years, the Historical Galleries have been tenderly attended to by specialists in preparation for a future presentation in the north and south wings.

Whether as the residence of the kings of France, the palace of the French republic, or a museum, the Versailles that reflects the breadth of French history remains a political symbol. Even now, France's National Assembly and Senate continue to meet in the south wing when discussing amendments to the French Constitution.

8
Léopold Delbeke (1866–?)
The Hall of Mirrors on the Evening of the Signature of the Treaty of Versailles, 28th June 1919
Oil on canvas, 91 × 73 m, North Attic

THE CHÂTEAU

THE CHÂTEAU OF VERSAILLES

Versailles, built on a narrow elevation, is revealed little by little to approaching visitors. After passing through the parade ground dominated by the equestrian statue of Louis XIV at its center, visitors progress through courtyards divided by gates. In this hierarchical space, you first see the Ministers' Wings and then the Gabriel Pavillon, built under the rule of Louis XV, and its duplicate on the left, the Dufour Pavillon, built during the Empire. The buildings reflect two hundred years of architecture. Under the Ancien Régime, the stately entranceway saw a lot of activity, with the comings and goings of the construction workers' carts and guards saluting the carriages of esteemed visitors. But only the king's carriage was authorized to pass beyond the royal gate, which was restored in 2008.

How modest the old château built around the Marble Court appears! This is the heart of the Versailles that Louis XIV preserved, consisting of roofs adorned with gilt-lead figures and facades embellished with columns, balconies, and ancient busts. The placement of the royal apartments is governed with rigorous symmetry: the king's to the north, the queen's to the south. The three sides of the building that surround the Marble Court have contained the interior apartment of the king since the end of the reign of Louis XIV. Behind this facade, Versailles never stopped growing and evolving, expanding to the size of a veritable city within the confines of the palace, as multiple floors and apartments contained within one another were constructed.

Facing the Marble Court, the Royal Chapel is located to the right in the north wing. Built from 1699 to 1710, it shows how Louis XIV's styles and tastes embraced the greater freedom of Baroque style. Inside, visitors are overwhelmed by dazzling light reflecting off white walls carved with delicate reliefs. The nave is surrounded by aisles surmounted by pews: Like all palatine chapels, the building features two majestic stories.

The iconography of the painted and sculptural decorations corresponds to a theological and political plan to demonstrate that the powers and the duties of the monarch are given by divine right: Beginning with the polychrome marble floor inscribed with St. Louis's monogram, there is a progression that rises to the arched ceiling. The reliefs on the pillars refer to the life of Christ and culminate with the *Dead Christ on the Knees of His Mother* located on the main altar. In the cornerstones, angels carrying the instruments of Christ's Passion form a bridge to the celestial level. The highly colorful paintings on the vault open out to a divine heaven filled with angels, evoking an entirely Italian sumptuousness with its blend of relief and trompe-l'oeil architecture. The Holy Trinity is depicted in a swirling setting: *God the Father in Glory* in the center, *The Resurrection of Christ* above the altar, and *The Pentecoste* dead center of the *tribune royale*, where the king and members of the royal family would sit during mass.

Under the Ancien Régime, the chapel was a place of devotion as well as a place for court spectacle, as the king attended mass every day. It served as the setting for baptisms, princely weddings, and major religious celebrations. Situated directly opposite the *tribune royale*, the organ reminds us that music was an important element of the palace's liturgical ceremonies; such celebrated composers as Michel Richard Delalande, François Couperin, and Marc-Antoine Charpentier were also chapel masters.

At the northernmost point of this wing, we find the Royal Opera. The choice of this location was part of the larger plan from the very beginning. But it was not until the announcement of the wedding of the Dauphin, the future Louis XVI, to Marie Antoinette, that Louis XV finally decided to complete the building. Responsibility for the construction was entrusted to the architect, Ange-Jacques Gabriel, and to Blaise-Henri Arnoult, the machinist of the *Menus Plaisirs du Roi* (Royal Entertainment of the King), an organization responsible for designing and orchestrating various ceremonies and entertainment, including plays, concerts, and ballets. Arnoult invented an ingenious mechanism that made it possible to elevate the floor of the orchestra's seating area so it was level with the stage, thus making it possible to transform the structure into a ballroom or a banqueting hall; in fact, this configuration was utilized during the wedding festivities in May 1770.

The Royal Opera, built in wood, was completed with astonishing speed, in less than two years. The simplicity of the structure and the perfection of the proportions are remarkable.

The decoration is relatively sober: A multitude of bas-reliefs and gilt medallions glitter on wooden walls painted in a faux marble pattern in shades of gray-green and pink. Guibert and Rousseau did the ornamentation, while Augustin Pajou was responsible for the bas-reliefs. On the top floor, arcades of mirrors enlarge the space, further magnified by a colonnade. With its French-style boxes, which are far more open to prying eyes than those of Italian theaters, the spectator sees while also being seen. However, for himself, Louis XV opted for three small, gated boxes that were more private and comfortable.

While the Royal Opera was not used extensively under the Ancien Régime, on October 1, 1789, a banquet was thrown here that the revolutionaries considered to be a provocation. The counterrevolutionary spirit of the gathering was one of the events that provoked the march to Versailles that resulted in the removal of the royal family to Paris on October 5, 1789.

The Royal Opera was used repeatedly during the nineteenth century and in 1837, in particular, for the inauguration of the Historical Galleries under Louis Philippe. He had the Royal Opera painted red with a gold harlequin pattern. It was also used for the banquet given by Napoleon III in honor of Queen Victoria on August 25, 1855. The government of the new Third Republic moved the Chamber, as the National Assembly was then known, to that hall. Its restoration began in 1952.

9
Pierre Cartellier (1757–1831) and **Louis Petitot** (1794–1862)
Equestrian Statue of Louis XIV, 1816–1836
Bronze, 530 × 240 cm, Parade Ground

10
The Palace of Versailles Seen from the Court of Honor
The fence was restored in 2008
by the architect Frédéric Didier.
Left statue: Antoine Coysevox (1640–1720)
Plenty, 1680–1681, stone, ca. 250 cm
Right statue: Jean-Baptiste Tuby (1635–1700)
Peace, 1680–1683, stone, ca. 250 cm

11
The Old Palace Seen from the Royal Court, 1624–1680
Philibert Le Roy († 1646) and Louis Le Vau (1610–1670)

12
The Marble Court, 1624–1680
Louis Le Vau (1610–1670)

13

13
Henri Chapu (1833–1891), after François Girardon (1628–1715)
Hercules Resting
and after Gaspard Marsy (1629–1681)
Mars Resting
Allegories of Louis XIV Victorious, 1869
Stone, 309 × 192.2 cm
Clock, 1678–1680, mechanism by Pierre Le Roy
Head of Apollo, 1680, gilt bronze
Dial, 1869, designed by Charles-Auguste Questel (1807–1888)
Painted copper and gilt bronze

14
After Benoît Massou (1633–1684)
Asia, stone, 180 × 140 m
and Léon Charpentier, after Pierre Legros (1629–1714),
Europe, stone, 175 × 145 cm
Copies executed in 1888–1889 after an original executed in 1678–1679

15
Étienne Le Hongre (1628–1690), *Africa* (left)
Thomas Regnaudin (1622–1706), *America* (right), 1678–1679
Stone, 260 cm

14

15

16
The Grand Stable with the Riding Pavilion
Jules Hardouin-Mansart (1646–1708)
Pediment of the central portal
Pierre Granier (1635–1715) and Jean Raon (1630–1707)
Cartouche carried by two Fames, 1680–1682
Stone and painted copper, 220 × 780 cm
Horses, 1680–1682, stucco, 240 × 480 cm
Four trophies of French-style jousts
and tournaments, 1680–1682, stone

17

17
Gallery of the Grand Court of the Grand Stable, 1680–1682
Jules Hardouin-Mansart (1646–1708)

18
Horses, 1680–1682
Pierre Granier (1635–1715) and Jean Raon (1630–1707)
Stucco, 240 × 480 cm, Grand Stable

1

19
The Royal Chapel, 1699–1710
Jules Hardouin-Mansart (1646–1708)
and Robert de Cotte (1656–1735)

20

20
Main Altar of the Royal Chapel
Corneille Van Cleve (1646–1732)
Retable: *Glory Surrounded by Angels*, 1709–1710, gilt bronze
Altar hanging: *Mourning over the Dead Christ*, 1709–1710, gilt bronze relief, 61 × 219 cm

21
The Royal Chapel, 1699–1710
Jules Hardouin-Mansart (1646–1708)
and Robert de Cotte (1656–1735)

22
Antoine Coypel (1661–1722)
God Almighty in His Glory Bringing the World the Promise of Redemption
Central Part of the Vault over the Nave of the Royal Chapel
Oil on plaster, in situ

23
The Royal Opera, 1765–1770
Ange-Jacques Gabriel (1698–1782) and Blaise-Henri Arnault

24
The Royal Opera, 1765–1770
Ange-Jacques Gabriel (1698–1782) and Blaise-Henri Arnault

25

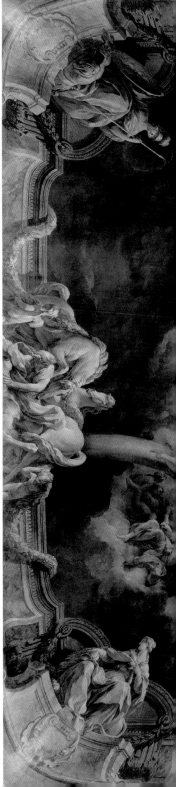

25
The Drawing Room of Hercules, 1722
Robert de Cotte (1656–1735) and
Jacques Gabriel (1667–1742)
Bronze Capitals and Mantelpiece, Antoine Vassé (1681–1736)
Paolo Caliari, also known as Veronese (1528–1588)
Eliezer and Rebecca (*Rebecca at the Well*), after 1550, oil on canvas, 366 × 240 cm
Gilded-wood frame, Jacques Verberckt (1704–1771)

26
François Lemoyne (1688–1737)
Apotheosis of Hercules, 1733–1736
Oil on canvas

26

27
Paolo Caliari, also known as Veronese (1528–1588)
Feast in the House of Simon, 1576
Oil on canvas, 474 × 974 cm
Gilded-wood Frame, Antoine Vassé (1681–1736)

THE KING'S GRAND APARTMENT

The apartments of the king and the queen, linked by the Hall of Mirrors, are on the upper floor, overlooking the gardens. Preceded by the Hercules Drawing Room, which was added during the reign of Louis XV, and by the Drawing Room of Plenty, which offered access to the Cabinet of Curiosities, the King's Grand Apartment has views of the north parterre. It is made up of an enfilade of antechambers and drawing rooms: the Diana Drawing Room and the Venus Drawing Room at the top of the Ambassadors' Staircase, the Mars Drawing Room, the Mercury Drawing Room or *Chambre de Parade*, and last of all, the Apollo Drawing Room or throne room.

The ceiling panels, painted from 1671 to 1680, were the work of leading artists of the French Academy under the supervision of Charles Le Brun, *Premier Peintre du Roi* (First Painter to His Majesty). Panels framed in gilt stucco are devoted to the myth of the sun with the planets depicted as the gods of Olympus, while the vaults portray exemplary acts of antiquity. The iconography is based on the Apartment of the Planets in the

Palazzo Pitti in Florence: "Just as the sun is the emblem of the king," wrote André Félibien, "it was decided to make the seven planets the subject of the panel paintings in the seven rooms of that apartment; as a result, in each room, it was necessary to depict the acts of the heroes of antiquity, placing them in relationship to each of the planets and the acts of his majesty."* No expense was spared, and the laws of symmetry were imposed right down to the gilded double doors, the marble, and the exquisite curtains, signaling the economic importance of the luxury industry and the skills of French craftsmen.

In 1678, Louis XIV decided to connect the royal apartments by means of the Hall of Mirrors, which was flanked by the War Salon to the north and the Peace Salon to the south. This vast passageway, conceived by Jules Hardouin-Mansart, opens to the west in seventeen bays, matched on the interior wall by seventeen mirrored arcades. The walls are sheathed in polychrome marble and adorned with gilt bronze trophies; the pillars and the columns are topped by columns of the French order, featuring a head of Apollo, a fleur-de-lis, and two roosters, all symbols of France. On the ceiling, the large canvases by Le Brun celebrate the greatest deeds of the early years of the reign of Louis XIV. The glow of gold overwhelms with its incomparable pomp.

An obligatory route for the kings of France who went each morning to the Royal Chapel, the Hall of Mirrors was also the location of the most sumptuous receptions and fetes. Indeed, Louis XIV did not inhabit that ceremonial apartment, but instead opened it to his court, which he normally received during the *soirées d'appartement* (evenings in the apartments), on Mondays, Wednesdays, and Thursdays from six o'clock until ten o'clock in the evening, and more importantly, on special occasions for receptions held for emissaries from distant kingdoms such as Siam, Morocco, and Persia.

* André Félibien, *Description sommaire du palace de Versailles*, Paris, G. Desprez, 1674.

28
Enfilade View of the King's Grand Apartment
from the Drawing Room of Plenty, 1678–1682

29

29
The Drawing Room of Plenty

30
René-Antoine Houasse (1645–1710)
The Nef of Louis XIV, 1686
Oil on plaster, detail of the ceiling of the Drawing Room of Plenty

32

31
Jacques Rousseau (1631–1693)
Trompe-l'oeil Perspective Framed by Ionic Columns, 1679–1680
Oil on canvas, 400 × 300 cm, Venus Drawing Room

32
The Venus Drawing Room

33

33
Diana Drawing Room

34
Marcus Aurelius
Ancient Roman Sculpture
Marble, 96 × 70 cm, Diana Drawing Room

34

35
Gian Lorenzo Bernini (1598–1680)
Bust of Louis XIV, 1665
Marble, 106 × 196 × 43 cm, Diana Drawing Room

36

36
The Mars Drawing Room

37
Claude II Audran (1639–1684)
The Chariot of Mars
Oil on canvas, Mars Drawing Room

38

38
Charles Le Brun (1619–1690)
The Family of Darius at the Feet of Alexander the Great, 1660–1661
Oil on canvas, 298 × 453 cm, Mars Drawing Room

39
Charles André, called Carle Van Loo (1705–1765)
Portrait of Marie Leszczynska
Oil on canvas, 274 × 193 cm, Drawing Room of 1747

40
Charles André, called Carle Van Loo (1705–1765)
Portrait of Louis XV
Oil on canvas, 277 × 183 cm, Mars Drawing Room

41
The Mercury Drawing Room
Clock with Automata, 1706, Antoine Morand (1674–1757)
Rosewood, sandalwood, and chased gilt bronze, 175 × 82 cm
Canopy and Head of the Bed, nineteenth century, gilt wood
Bedspread, seventeenth century, needlepoint embroidery in a Saint Cyr stitch

41

75

42
Jean-Baptiste de Champaigne (1631–1681)
Center: *The Chariot of Mercury,* oil on canvas
Left arch: *Alexander the Great Receiving Ethiopian Envoys,* oil on canvas
Center arch: *Ptolemy Philadelphus in the Library of Alexandria,* oil on canvas
Right arch: *Augustus Receiving Indian Envoys,* oil on canvas
Mercury Drawing Room

43
The Apollo Drawing Room
Pierre-Edme Babel and Toussaint Foliot (ca. 1715–1798),
after Jacques Gondoin (1737–1818)
Pedestal Tables of the Hall of Mirrors, 1769, carved gilt oak

44
Charles de La Fosse (1636–1716)
The Chariot of Apollo
Oil on canvas, 490 cm in diameter

45
The War Drawing Room, 1678–1784
Jules Hardouin-Mansart (1646–1708) and
Charles Le Brun (1619–1690)
Polychrome marbles, trophies in gilt bronze, mirrors from the Manufactory of Saint-Gobain
Antoine Coysevox (1640–1720)
Louis XIV Victorious Crowned by Glory, 1681–1716, stucco relief
Trophies and Reliefs of the Gilt Bronze trumeaux
Pierre Ladoireau (active from 1679–1716)
Clio Writing the History of the King, bas-relief covering the fireplace
Ancient Busts of Roman Emperors

48

46 | 47
The Hall of Mirrors, 1678–1684
Jules Hardouin-Mansart (1636–1716)
and Charles Le Brun (1619–1690)
12.3 × 73 × 10.5 m
Torchères Draped with Girandoles
After drawings by Jacques Gondoin (1737–1818)

48
After Charles Le Brun (1619–1690)
Trophy of Military Victory and Putti
Hall of Mirrors

49
Putti and Flower Garlands
Paint on plaster, Hall of Mirrors

ÉTABLISSEMENT
DE L'HOSTEL ROYAL
DES INVALIDES
1674.

51
Vault of the Hall of Mirrors

LA FVREVR DES DVELS ARRESTÉE.1662.

54

52
Charles Le Brun (1619–1690)
The King Rules Alone (1661), 1681–1684
Oil on canvas, Hall of Mirrors

53
Charles Le Brun (1619–1690)
The Capture of the Town and Citadel of Ghent in Six Days in 1678, 1681–1684
Oil on canvas, Hall of Mirrors

50
Charles Le Brun (1619–1690)
The Foundation of the Hotel Royal Des Invalides in 1674, 1681–1684
Oil on plaster, Hall of Mirrors

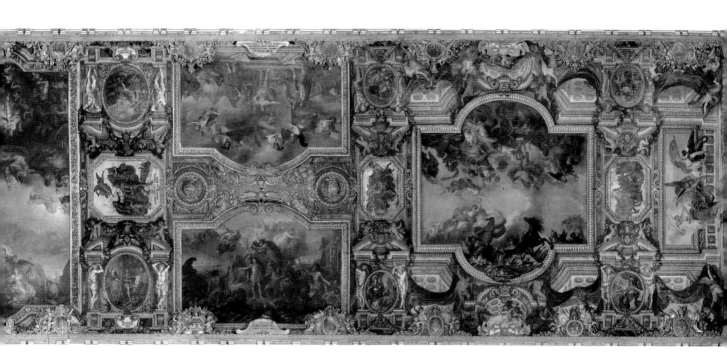

LA PAIX CONCLVE À AIX LA CHAPELLE
1668.

54
After Charles Le Brun (1619–1690)
Halting the Fury of Duels (1662), 1684
Hall of Mirrors

55
After Charles Le Brun (1619–1690)
The Making of Peace at Aix-la-Chapelle (1668), 1684
Hall of Mirrors

THE QUEEN'S APARTMENT

The Queen's Apartment is reached by the Queen's Staircase, also known as the Marble Staircase. This was the most heavily trafficked staircase during the Ancien Régime because it also provided access to the King's Grand Apartment. Entirely decorated with polychrome marble, the staircase runs up to a landing covered with a loggia; there, visitors stand face-to-face with painted figures in front of trompe-l'oeil architecture. This is the path that the rioters took on October 6, 1789, before breaking into the room of Queen Marie Antoinette.

The apartment overlooks the flowered *Parterre du Midi*, or southern parterre. Its floor plan resembles that of the *Grand Appartement du Roi*, or King's Grand Apartment, to which it is symmetrical. The living space of the queens Maria Theresa, Marie Leszczynska, and Marie Antoinette included the marble-decorated guard room crafted during the reign of Louis XIV, the Antechamber of the *Grand Couvert*, the *Salon des Nobles*, and the bedroom.

In the antechamber, the queen and the king dined "*au grand couvert*," that is to say, in public, a ceremony that did not change until the French Revolution. The *Salon des Nobles* (or Drawing Room of the Nobles) served as an audience hall and meeting place for the ladies of the court. In June 1785, it was renovated in the latest fashion by the architect Richard Mique, who replaced the wainscoting with a wall hanging in apple-green damask fringed with gold braid.

The bedroom's decoration bears the marks of its three occupants. Beneath the gilt monograms of Maria Theresa and Louis XIV are carved wood panels created for Marie Leszczynska by Jacques Verbeckt, begun in 1725 under the supervision of the architect Ange-Jacques Gabriel. Four paintings in grisaille by François Boucher depict the virtues of the queen: abundance, fidelity, prudence, and charity. Marie Antoinette added portraits of her mother, her brother, and King Louis XVI; she also ordered a new curtain of silk damask with a white ground brocaded with bouquets of lilacs and peacock plumes. As in the king's residence, a gilt wooden balustrade separates the public area from the more private alcove. Aside from its chief function, the queens also used this room to receive ladies of the court, allowing them private audiences.

On either side of the bed, two nearly invisible doors allowed the queen to withdraw into the rooms that surrounded the apartment. The windows of these small rooms overlooked courtyards, therefore lacking both views and space, but it is evident that particular care was taken with the decoration, where luxury competes with exquisite delicacy. Marie Antoinette gave Richard Mique responsibility for revamping the look of the Gilt Drawing Room with its Greek motifs; the Library of the Queen, also gilded; and the Méridienne (or Cabinet of the Meridian, which may have indicated its use during midday hours). The carved wood motifs in this room, where Marie Antoinette particularly liked to spend her leisure time, celebrate the birth of the Dauphin. The garland of roses sculpted in stucco is elegantly echoed in the glass of the doors.

56
The Peace Drawing Room, 1678–1686
Jules Hardouin-Mansart (1646–1708)
and Charles Le Brun (1619–1690)
François Lemoyne (1688–1737)
Louis XV Offering Peace to Europe, 1729
Oil on canvas, 382 × 295 cm

57
The Queen's Staircase, 1680
Polychrome marble, stone steps
Philippe Meusnier (1655–1734), Charles François Poerson (1653–1725)
and Jean-Baptiste Blain, called Blin de Fontenay (1653–1715)
Perspective View of a Palace with Characters Dressed in Oriental Style
Oil on canvas, 380 × 405 cm

58

58
Loggia of the Queen's Staircase, 1701

59
Benoît Massou (1627–1684)
Allegory of the Wedding of Louis XIV and Maria Theresa of Austria, 1681
Gilt lead

60

60
Hall of the Queen's Guards, 1680

61
Noël Coypel (1628–1707)
Female Figure
Oil on plaster, detail of the northeast corner of the arches of the Hall of the Queen's Guards

62
Antechamber of the Queen's *Grand Couvert*
Silverware Service of George III of England, 1776–1777
Robert-Joseph Auguste (1723–1805), silver, Paris
(some of the pieces are the property of the Musée du Louvre)
Six Panels of a Folding Screen, turn the eighteenth century,
after Jean-Baptiste Blain, called Blin de Fontenay (1653–1715)
Manufactory of the Savonnerie
Pendulum Clock, Louis XVI period
Chased gilt bronze, violet wood veneer, movement by Étienne Lenoir

63
Élisabeth Vigée Lebrun (1755–1842)
Queen Marie Antoinette and Her Children, 1787
Oil on canvas, 275 × 215 cm, Antechamber of the Queen's *Grand Couvert*

64

64
Chest of Drawers, 1786
Jean-Henri Riesener (1734–1806)
Mahogany, gilt bronze, 101 × 202 × 70.3 cm

65
Michel II Corneille (1642–1708)
Mercury, the Arts and the Sciences, 1672
Oil on canvas, central section of the ceiling of the Drawing Room of the Nobles

66
Bedroom of the Queen, 1730–1735
Decoration done under the supervision of Robert de Cotte (1656–1735)
and Jacques Gabriel (1667–1742)
Boiserie and Mirror Frames, Jules Degoullons (1671–1737)
André Le Goupil, and Jacques Verberckt (1704–1771)
Portrait of Joseph II, tapestry
Jewel Box, 1787, Ferdinand Schwerdfeger (1734–1818)
Mahogany, mother-of-pearl, and gilt bronze, 265 × 200 × 0.65 cm
Screen, 1787, Jean-Baptiste Claude Sené (1748–1803)
Carved gilt walnut, brocaded white grosgrain cloth, 126.5 × 77 × 40.3 cm

68

67
Lit à la duchesse (Bed)
From the Desfarges atelier in Lyon,
Done to drawings by Jean-François Bony (1764–1826)
Bedspread, 1786–1787, Félix Lecomte (1737–1817)
Silk and grosgrain, brocaded and embroidered with bouquets and ribbons, 275 × 220 cm,
Bedroom of the Queen

68
Félix Lecomte (1737–1817)
Bust of Marie Antoinette, 1783
Marble, 86 × 50 × 28 cm, Bedroom of the Queen

70

71

69
Boiseries of the Bedroom of the Queen, 1730–1735
Jules Degoullons (1671–1737), André Le Goupil,
and Jacques Verberckt (1704–1771)
Done to drawings by Robert de Cotte (1656–1735)
and Jacques Gabriel (1667–1742)
Charles Joseph Natoire (1700–1777)
Youth and Virtue Introduce
Madame Adelaide and Madame Louise to France, 1735
Oil on canvas, 115 × 146 cm, overdoor of the Bedroom of the Queen

70
François Boucher (1703–1770)
Pity, 1735
Oil on canvas, grisaille, ceiling arch of the Bedroom of the Queen

71
François Boucher (1703–1770)
Charity, 1735
Oil on canvas, grisaille, ceiling arch of the Bedroom of the Queen

73

72
The Salon Doré or The Queen's Grand Interior Apartment, 1783
Richard Mique (1728–1794)
Armchair, 1779, François Foliot
Circular Footstool, 1783, Georges Jacob (1739–1814)

73
Boiserie of the Salon Doré
Jules-Hugues (1743–1806) and Jean-Siméon (1747–1820) Rousseau,
after Richard Mique (1728–1794)
Detail

74

75
Painted Woodwork
of the Cabinet of the Poets

Detail

74
The Cabinet of the Poets of Marie Leszczynska

76

76
Book Belonging to Marie Antoinette, *Le Théâtre de la foire*
Bound in dappled calfskin featuring the coat of arms of Queen Marie Antoinette
Crowned *CT* (Château de Trianon) at the bottom of the spine
Library of the Queen

77
The Library of the Queen, 1772–1779
Richard Mique (1728–1794)

78
The Cabinet of the Meridian, 1781
Richard Mique (1728–1794)
Boiserie, Jules-Hugues (1743–1806) and
Jean-Siméon (1747–1820) Rousseau
Pedestal table, 1770
Setting by Anton Domanöck (1713–1739)
Vienna, petrified wood set on steel and gilt bronze, 86.7 × 72.6 × 55.5 cm
Armchair, Georges Jacob (1739–1814)

79
Bathroom
Lit à la Polonaise (Bed), 1785
Jean-Baptiste Boulard (ca. 1730–1789)
Carved painted beechwood, 141.3 × 204 × 129.7 cm

80
Élisabeth Vigée Lebrun (1755–1842)
Portrait of Marie Thérèse Charlotte of France and Her Brother,
the Dauphin Louis Joseph Xavier, 1784
Oil on canvas, 132 × 94 cm

131

81
Hubert Robert (1733–1808)
View of the Green Carpet at Versailles, 1775–1777
Oil on canvas, 124 × 191 cm

THE KING'S INTERIOR APARTMENTS

Was it in order to perfect the ceremonies of the *Lever* and the *Coucher*—in which attendants surrounded the king when he woke up and when he went to sleep—that Louis XIV placed his bedchamber at the central axis of the château in 1701? The room where the king slept became the nucleus of the residence and, therefore, of the kingdom. After the death of his son, the Grand Dauphin, followed by the death of his grandson, the Duke of Burgundy, and then by the death of the eldest of his great-grandsons, the Duke of Brittany, the crown fell to the Duke of Anjou—the future Louis XV—who was five years old when Louis XIV died on September 1, 1715.

When he returned to Versailles after the Regency, the new king adapted his grandfather's apartment to his own taste. The bedchamber became a ceremonial room, where the *Lever* would still take place, while Louis XV set up his actual bedroom a few yards away. Etiquette was a veritable chronometer that governed Versailles at all hours of the day and night and accentuated the similarities between one reign and another—the king never really dies—but distinctive differences between the two rooms divided the persona of the king, introducing the notion that a ruler might have a private life.

Under Louis XV, the Council Study was expanded; the new woodwork motifs—trophies of peace and war, attributes of the army, the navy, and of justice, the insignia of the monarchy—are all evocative of the government and its triumphs. He then ordered the construction of the semicircular staircase that adjoins the Grand Gallery, making it possible to go downstairs where the apartments of his mistresses, Madame de Pompadour and Madame du Barry, were located.

After creating the *Cabinet des Chiens*, or Antechamber of Dogs, in 1738, where the king's favorite dogs were allowed to sleep, and the *Salle à Manger des Retours de Chasse* (the After-Hunt Dining Room), Louis XV worked on the enfilade of rooms overlooking the Marble Court. The enfilade included the *Cabinet de la Pendule*, or clock room, and the luxurious corner room, or interior study of the king, a room that housed a rolltop desk commissioned from cabinetmaker Jean-François Œben but completed by Riesener in 1769.

Louis XVI was content with this arrangement and made few modifications to the king's interior apartments. It was in this setting that on March 20, 1778, he received, in a solemn audience, Benjamin Franklin and the American diplomats who had come to sign a treaty of friendship and commerce between France and the United States. The working study also served as a good location for discretely receiving those whom the king preferred not to introduce into the *Cabinet du Conseil* (Council Room), such as the Cardinal de Rohan during the "affair of the necklace" in 1785.

The smaller dimensions of these rooms testify to the king's love for intimacy; the walls are covered with woodcarvings created by Antoine Rousseau or Jacques Verbeckt from drawings by the architect Ange-Jacques Gabriel. The introduction of mirrors above the mantelpiece and facing one another increased the sense of refinement; the frames of the mirrors carved in foliage and trelliswork, and in some cases in busts of women, are delicately animated by a rococo spirit that broke away from the more ostentatious order of the previous century. Yet a certain splendor still preserves the sense of hierarchy and dignity.

Louis XVI also showed a special predilection for small spaces by ordering the renovation of the dressing room that overlooks the Courtyard of the Stags. Its woodwork, carved by the Rousseau brothers, feature characteristics of commerce, agriculture, navigation, war, the sciences, and the arts, mixed with arabesques, rose foliage and animal heads. He also built the *Cabinet de la Cassette* (or privy purse room), where he installed his private ledgers in the former bath chamber of Louis XV, while the bedchamber of Madame Adélaïde became an immense library, indicating the king's love of study. The new rooms built at the base of the Ambassadors' Staircase terminate at the dining room, whose carved wooden panels, the work of Verbeckt, were completed in 1769.

82

83

82
The Antechamber of the Bull's Eye, 1701
Jules Hardouin-Mansart (1646–1708)
and Robert de Cotte (1656–1735)

83
Arch of the Antechamber of the Bull's Eye, 1701
Poulletier, Hardy, Simon Hurtrelle (1648–1724),
Corneille Van Cleve (1646–1732) and Flamen
Gilt stucco

84
Jean Nocret (1617–1672)
The Family of Louis XIV Portrayed as Mythological Creatures, 1670
Oil on canvas, 305 × 420 cm, Antechamber of the Bull's Eye

85
The King's Bedchamber, 1701

86
Nicolas Coustou (1658–1733)
Allegory of France Watching over the King's Sleep, 1701
Gilt plaster, King's Bedchamber

87
Anton Van Dyck (1599–1641)
Portrait of François de Moncade
Oil on canvas, 68 × 58 cm, King's Bedchamber

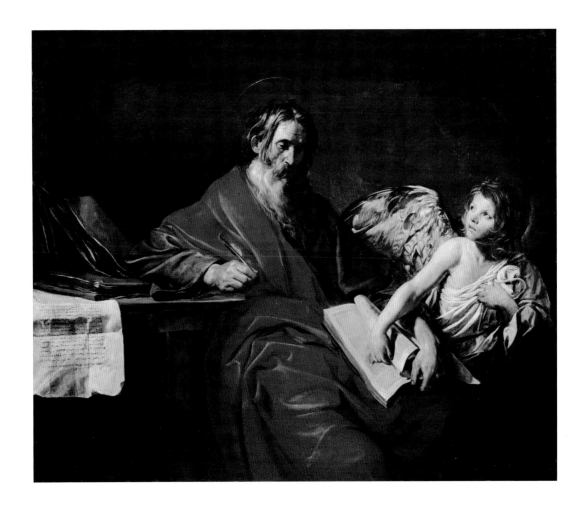

88
Valentin de Boulogne (1594–1632)
Saint Matthew
Oil on canvas, 120 × 146 cm, King's Bedchamber

89
Valentin de Boulogne (1594–1632)
Saint Mark
Oil on canvas, 120 × 146 cm, King's Bedchamber

90
Antique statue restored and completed by **François Girardon** (1628–1715)
Alexander the Great, additions ca. 1699
Porphyry, marble, and gilt bronze, 114.5 × 74 × 103.5 cm, *Cabinet du Conseil* (Council Room)

91
The New Bedchamber, or Bedchamber of Louis XV
and Louis XVI, 1738
Gold-brocaded damasked silk
Workshop of Jean-Marc Nattier (1685–1756)
Madame Adelaide de France Holding a Book of Sheet Music
Oil on canvas, 105 × 120 cm

92

93

92 | 93
Wainscoting of the Dressing-Room of the Wardrobe of Louis XVI, 1788
Jules-Hugues (1743–1806) and Jean-Siméon (1747–1820) Rousseau
Wardrobe of Louis XVI

94
Jules-Hugues (1743–1806) and Jean-Siméon (1747–1820) Rousseau
The Attributes of Agriculture and *The Attributes of Commerce*, 1788
Wardrobe of Louis XVI

96

95
Astronomical Pendulum Clock, 1749–1753
Claude Siméon Passemant (1702–1769), Louis Dauthiau (1730–1809),
Jacques (1678–1755) and Philippe (1714–1774) Caffieri
Gilt bronze, enamel, steel, copper, and glass, 206 × 83.2 × 53 cm, Dressing Room of the Pendulum Clock

96
Dressing Room of the Pendulum Clock
Louis-Claude Vassé (1716–1772),
after Edme Bouchardon (1698–1762)
Copy of the equestrian statue of Louis XV, bronze

98

99

97
The After-Hunt Dining Room, 1752–1754
Wainscoting, Jules-Antoine Rousseau (1710–1782)
Done to drawings by Ange-Jacques Gabriel (1698–1782)
Mantelpiece, Louis Trouard, purple breccia marble
Barometer, 1770–1772, Jean-Joseph Lemaire (1740–ca. 1820)

98
After Edme Jeurat (1688–1738)
Woman Holding a Child, 1775
Porcelain, Sèvres Porcelain Manufactory, After-Hunt Dining Room

99
After Jean Barbault (1718–1762)
Hunter Priming His Rifle, 1774–1775
Porcelain, Sèvres Porcelain Manufactory, After-Hunt Dining Room

100
The Interior Study
Mirror Frames, 1738, and Wainscoting, 1753, Jacques Verberckt (1704–1771)
Cylinder Secretaire, 1760–1769, Jean-François Œben (1720–1763),
Jean-Henri Riesener (1734–1806), and David Roetgen (1743–1807), 147.3 × 192.5 × 105 cm
Clock, 1769, Jean-Antoine Lépine (1720–1814)

101

101
Medal Cabinet, 1739, Antoine-Robert Gaudreaus (ca. 1682–1746), and
Sébastien-Antoine (1695–1754) and Paul-Ambroise (1702–1758) Slodtz
Violetwood veneer, medallions of the cabinet doors on a tortoiseshell background with gilt bronze, 92.7 × 172.2 × 64 cm
Two Vases
Porcelain and gilt bronze, Sèvres Porcelain Manufactory
Candelabrum of American Independence, 1783
Pierre-Philippe Thomire (1751–1843)
Chased gilt bronze, Interior Study

102
Wainscoting, Jacques Verberckt (1704–1771)
Encoignure (corner cabinet), 1755
Gilles Joubert (1689–1775)
Violet wood veneer, gilt bronze, 935 × 102 × 77 cm
Interior Study

103
La pièce de la Vaisselle d'or, or Room of the Gold Table Service
Wainscoting, 1753–1767, Jacques Verberckt (1704–1771),
after Jacques-Anges Gabriel (1698–1782)
Antoine Coysevox (1640–1720)
Bust of Louis XV as a Child, ca. 1719
Marble, 66.5 × 50 × 20.5 cm
Medal Cabinet, Guillaume Benneman (?–1811)
Oak, mahogany, ebony, wax, butterfly wings, plants, feathers
Bronzes, attributed to Pierre-Philippe Thomire (1751–1843) and François Rémond (1747–1812)
101 × 82 × 39 cm

105

106

104
The Bath Room of Louis XV, 1771
Jules-Antoine (1710–1782),
Jules-Hugues (1743–1806),
and Jean-Siméon (1747–1820) Rousseau,
after Ange-Jacques Gabriel (1698–1782)
Writing Table, 1756
Jean-François Œben (1720–1763)
and Gilles Joubert

105
Young Girls Playing in a River, 1771
Jules-Antoine (1710–1782),
Jules-Hugues (1743–1806),
and Jean-Siméon (1747–1820) Rousseau,
after Ange-Jacques Gabriel (1698–1782)
Bas-relief medallion in the boiserie of the Bath Room

106
Venus, 1771
Jules-Antoine (1710–1782),
Jules-Hugues (1743–1806),
and Jean-Siméon (1747–1820) Rousseau,
after Ange-Jacques Gabriel (1698–1782)
Bas-relief medallion in the boiserie of the Bath Room

107
The Library of Louis XVI, 1774
Ange-Jacques Gabriel (1698–1782)
Allegory of France, above the mirror
Globe of the Earth and **Globe of the Sky,** 1777
Pierre Lartigue (1745–1826) and Louis Lennel (1740–1784)
Bronzed plaster, 152 × 58 cm
Chest of Drawers, 1778, Jean-Henri Riesener (1734–1806)
Inlaid marquetry of purpleheart, sycamore, tulipwood, satinwood, maple, and
mahogany, gilt bronze, variegated Sarancolin Pyrenees marble, 95 × 165 × 63 cm

109

108
The Dining Room in the New Halls or
The Dining Room of the Porcelains, 1769
Ange-Jacques Gabriel (1698–1782)
Table, 1785–1786, Jean-François Limonne, Mahogany, 73 × 345.5 × 269 cm
Chairs, Jean-Baptiste Boulard (1725–1789) and
Jean-Baptiste Claude Sené (1748–1803)
Molded painted beechwood, 95 × 52.5 × 56 cm

109
Nicolas Pierre Pithou (active from 1757–1790),
after Jean-Baptiste Oudry (1686–1755)
The Hunt of Louis XVI: The Stag Crosses the River Oise on the Royalieu Side,
Within Sight of the Town of Compiègne, 1779
Painting done on soft porcelain, Manufactory of Sèvres, 39 × 49 cm,
Dining Room in the New Halls

110
Louis Nicolas van Blarenberghe (1716–1794)
The Siege of Oudenarde from July 17th to 21st, 1745, 1788
Gouache on vellum stretched over cardboard, 61.2 × 95.6 cm

111
Louis Nicolas van Blarenberghe (1716–1794)
The Siege of Brussels from the 7th to the 20th of February, 1746, 1781
Gouache on vellum stretched over cardboard, 60 × 94.7 cm

112
The Bedroom of the Marquise de Pompadour
Bed, attributed to Louis Delanois
Chest of Drawers, Léonard Boudin
Burgundian table

113
The Grand Apartment of the Marquise de Pompadour

114
The Grand Apartment of the Comtesse du Barry
Mirrored Alcove, 1770

115
After Augustin Pajou
Bust of the Comtesse du Barry
Tinted plaster, nineteenth-century cast, 72 × 48 × 24 cm

116
The Bedroom of the Comtesse du Barry

15

117
The Marble Vestibule

THE APARTMENTS OF THE PRINCES

During the Ancien Régime, the ground floor of the central structure was occupied by the apartments of the princes. For instance, during the rule of Louis XV, the Dauphin Louis-Ferdinand, the king's son and the heir to the throne, and the Dauphine Maria Josepha of Saxony, the daughter-in-law of kings, had their apartments on the south side, while Mesdames, the daughters of Louis XV, lived on the north side.

The princely couple occupied a double apartment, and the future Louis XVI, the Duc de Berry, with his wife Marie Antoinette, later occupied this same space. In keeping with the traditional arrangement, the enfilade includes a guardroom, a first and second antechamber, a bedchamber, and the large study. An interior study with wainscoting carved with delicate raised garlands is the last room in the Dauphine's apartment that connects to the elegant Library of the Dauphin, which contains exceptional decorations created by the architect, Ange-Jacques Gabriel. The wood panels are decorated with trophies and brightly colored garlanded flowers, while mirrors lighten and enlarge the space.

In 1769, Adélaïde and Victoire, two of Louis XV's daughters, took up residence on the other side of the ground floor of the central structure. Madame Victoire occupied the former Apartment of the Baths of Louis XIV and enjoyed a first antechamber, a second antechamber (or noble room) a large corner study, and a bedroom, followed by an interior study and a library that connected with the apartment of Madame Adélaïde. The decoration of Victoire's apartment is elegant; the wood carvings of the bedchamber and of the interior study, created by Antoine Rousseau, are crowned by a finely sculpted cornice. The apartment of Madame Adélaïde, the former residence of the Marquise de Pompadour, includes a large study, a bedchamber, and an interior study.

118
The Bedroom of the Dauphin, 1747
Boiserie, Jacques Verberckt (1704–1771) after Ange-Jacques Gabriel (1698–1782)
Lit à la duchesse (Bed), ca. 1740
Bedspread embroidered in a Saint Cyr stitch
Bronzes on the Griotte Marble Mantelpiece
Jacques (1678–1755) and Philippe (1714–1774) Caffieri
Armchair, ca. 1740, attributed to Nicolas or Jean-Baptiste Tilliard, carved gilt wood
Armoire, Bernard II Van Risen Burgh (B.V.R.B., ca. 1696–before 1797)
Inlaid panels of red and gold Chinese lacquer

119
Globe Showing the Depths of the Seas and Oceans and the Vault of the Heavens, 1786
Edme Mentelle (1730–1815) and Jean Tobie Mercklein
Wood, cardboard, brass, iron, and stucco, 240 × 130 cm, Library of the Dauphin

120
Joseph Vernet (1714–1789)
The Storm, or Midday
Overdoor forming part of *The Four Times of Day*, 1762
Oil on canvas, 85 × 135 cm, Library of the Dauphin

121
The Library of the Dauphin
Boiseries, 1755, Jacques Verberckt (1704–1771),
after Ange-Jacques Gabriel (1698–1782)
Writing table, 1756, Simon Œben (?–1775), Roger Van der Cruse,
called Lacroix (1728–1799)
Veneer in satinwood and rosewood framed in purpleheart, gilt bronzes,
75.6 × 162.8 × 80.5 cm
Armchairs, Moscow, ca. 1750, attributed to Lazarev or
Sapojnikov, painted carved wood

122
François-Hubert Drouais (1727–1775)
Portrait of the Count of Artois with His Sister Marie-Clotilde-Xavière, 1763–1764
Oil on canvas, 119 × 97 cm

123
The Large Dressing Room of the Dauphine
Carpet from the Royal Manufactory of the Savonnerie
Writing Table, ca. 1720
Veneer in purpleheart, gilt bronzes
Barometer, 1773, Jean-Joseph Lemaire
Carved gilt wood

124
Bedchamber of the Dauphine, 1747
Lit à la polonaise (Bed), Nicolas Heurtaut (1720–1771)
Carved gilt walnut, upholstered in old damasked silk,
402 × 212.5 × 180 cm
Chest of Drawers, ca. 1740
Panels in polychrome lacquer on a black background and gilt bronze

125
The Interior Dressing Room of the Dauphine
Slant-front Writing Desk, 1745, Bernard II Van Risen Burgh (B.V.R.B., ca. 1696–before 1797)
Veneer in satinwood with purpleheart compartments and violet wood marquetry, gilt bronzework, 86.6 × 88.5 × 54 cm
Chest of Drawers, 1745, Antoine-Robert Gaudreaus (ca. 1682–1746)
Veneer in violet wood, gilt bronzework
Chairs, 1787, Jean-Baptiste Claude Sené
Chandelier, ca. 1750
Painted sheet metal and Dresden porcelain

126
Adélaïde Labille-Guiard (1749–1803)
Portrait of Marie-Thérèse-Louise-Victoire, Known As Madame Victoire, 1788
Oil on canvas, 271 × 165 cm

127
The Large Dressing Room of Madame Victoire

128
Olivier-Michel Barthélemy (1712–1784)
*English Tea Served in the Drawing Room of the Four Mirrors
in the Palais du Temple,* 1764
Oil on canvas, 53 × 68 cm

130

131

129
The Library of Madame Victoire
Armchairs (*Chaises à la Reine*) and
Chairs (*Chaise à carreau*), ca. 1755–1760
Nicolas-Quinibert Foliot (1706–1776)
Carved painted beechwood, 96 × 55 × 61.2 cm

130
Bookplate of Madame Victoire

131
Revolutionary Label from the Library of Madame Victoire

132
The Hall of the Hoquetons, or Guards

134

THE HISTORICAL GALLERIES

The construction project that transformed Versailles into a museum lasted fifteen years. For economic and symbolic reasons, the changes had little effect on the central structure. In contrast, significant changes were made to the two wings where Louis Philippe created the Historical Galleries.

From 1833 to 1837, the king demolished the apartments of the south wing, replacing them with the Hall of the Consulate and the Hall of the Empire on the ground floor, and the Hall of Battles upstairs. Then, from 1837 until the end of his reign, construction focused on the King's Pavilion in the north wing and the creation of the Hall of Crusades and the Hall of Africa. Each suite of rooms displays an array of wall paintings that express the king's desire to base his power on a foundation of national history; this area is flanked on the north and south by stone galleries adorned with statues. This conversion of Versailles established a decorative vocabulary, but one that was inherited from the Ancien Régime: In fact, the faux-marble wainscot paneling, wide symmetrical doors, and arched vaults painted in trompe-l'oeil reliefs are ornamentation evocative of the King's Grand Apartment (see page 54–95).

The most radical transformation was that of the Hall of Battles, which retraces French military history from the Battle of Tolbiac to the Battle of Wagram. As is often the case in Versailles, producing such a monumental space was the result of true technical prowess, where the walls and columns conceal a carefully designed metal framework permitting the construction of overhead skylights. Everything here endeavors to express symbolism; the architectural vocabulary is highly stylized, with the flourishes and ornaments of a timeless, elegant style that can slip into the conventional. The featured works speak in terms of metaphors and oppositions; they advocate a return to history. Versailles becomes a geopolitical location.

In the north wing, running from the Royal Chapel to the Royal Opera, the five Halls of the Crusades are built around the door of the Hospital of the Knights of Rhodes, which dates back to the fourteenth century. They were inaugurated in 1843 with neo-gothic furnishings in keeping with the historic spirit of the paintings.

In 1839, construction began on the upper floor in the Hall of Constantine, Hall of Morocco, and Hall of Louis Philippe, later called the Hall of Smalah, or the Smalah Room. A roof rises more than thirty feet high (nine meters high), and a traditional architectural style once again conceals a metal structure that supports a series of immense glass roofs. The panels and decoration of these rooms are the work of Horace Vernet, whose experiences in Algeria led to the creation of about twenty canvases for Versailles. But between *The Capture of Antwerp* and *The Capture of Abd-el-Kader's Smalah*, the subjects vary widely. What they have in common is the goal of celebrating the prestige of the French army.

These artworks are more ethnographic than military, because Vernet took care to deploy a number of pictorial anecdotes in the foreground. The proliferation of different scenes from different moments in history, the tangled welter of characters, and the attention to detail support the dramatic tension of these panoramic compositions. The canvases clearly offer a respectful bow to the patriotic spirit, but the style is more suited to the bivouac than to the battlefield. This triumph of everyday details over great deeds explains the indignant declamation of the Frères Goncourt in *Manette Salomon*: "Great talents who had made their reputation, who had enjoyed their day of inspiration and originality, deserted the field of art to become salaried laborers in that great museum of Versailles, which has proved so fatal to painting because of the official nature of its subjects and commissions, the haste demanded in terms of execution, all those projects undertaken on a job rate, made to measure, which were to convert the gallery of our glories into the school and the pantheon of bric-a-brac."

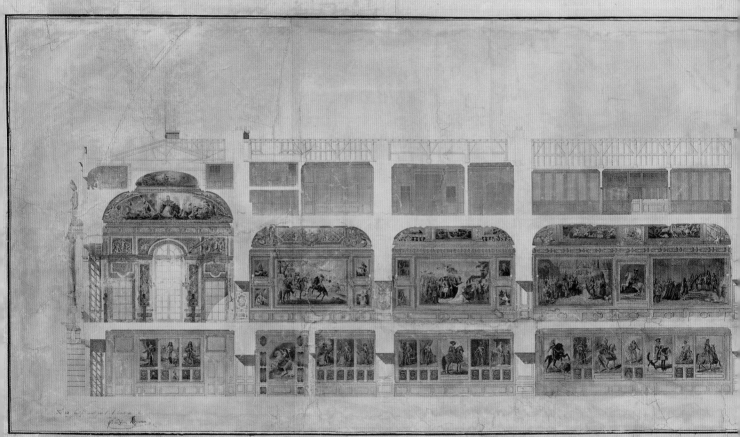

TRAVAUX ORDONNÉS PAR LE ROI POUR LA CONVERSION DU PALAIS DE

Coupe sur les salles des Maréchaux, des Amira

AILLES EN SALLES GALERIES ET MUSÉE HISTORIQUES

...nce de Appartements de la Reine. Principal-Corps.

135
Architectural Studio of Frédéric Nepveu (1777–1862)
View of the south side of the central structure with the enfilade of the Queen's Apartment
Ink and watercolor, ca. 1840

136
North Stone Gallery

137
Prosper Lafaye (1806–1883)
*Louis-Philippe, the Royal Family and King Leopold I Visiting the
Great "Salle des Croisades" at the Château de Versailles*, 1844
Oil on canvas, 60 × 85 cm, Hall of Crusades

138
Émile Signol (1804–1892)
The Crossing of the Bosphorus by
Godfrey of Bouillon in May 1097

Oil on canvas, 325 × 558 cm,
Drawing Room of 1855

139

Horace Vernet (1789–1863)

Battle of Las Navas de Tolosa in Which the Kings of Castile Defeat the Almohads, 16 July 1212

Oil on canvas, 406 × 492 cm, Drawing Room of 1817

140
Simon Vouet (1590–1649)
Louis XIII Between Female Figures Representing France and Navarre
Oil on canvas, 179 × 141 cm

141
French School
Louis XIV as a Child
Oil on canvas, 45 × 37 cm

142
Pierre Mignard (1612–1695)
The Family of Louis of France, called the Grand Dauphin, 1687
Oil on canvas, 232 × 304 cm

143
Antoine Benoist (1632–1717)
Portrait of Louis XIV, ca. 1705
Colored wax, fabric, and hair, 52 × 42 cm

144
Charles Le Brun (1619–1690)
Portrait of Henri de la Tour d'Auvergne, Vicomte de Turenne
Oil on canvas, 67 × 52 cm

145
Claude Lefebvre (1632–1675)
Portrait of Jean-Baptiste Colbert, 1666
Oil on canvas, 130 × 96 cm

146

146
Carlo Maratta (1625–1713)
Portrait of André Le Nôtre, 1679
Oil on canvas, 112 × 85 cm

147
Pierre Mignard (1612–1695)
Portrait of Françoise d'Aubigné, the Marquise of Maintenon,
in St. Frances of Rome, ca. 1694
Oil on canvas, 128 × 97 cm

147

148
Antoine Coypel (1661–1722)
The Moroccan Ambassador and His Entourage at the Italian Comedy in Paris in February 1682
Oil on canvas, 28 × 22 cm

149
Adam Frans Van der Meulen (1632–1690)
Solemn Entry of Louis XIV and Maria Theresa into Arras, 30th July 1667
Oil on canvas, 232 × 331 cm

150
Jean Garnier (1632–1705)
Portrait of Louis XIV among the Attributes of the Arts and Sciences, 1672
Oil on canvas, 163 × 204 cm

151
Gabriel Revel (1643–1712)
Portrait of the Sculptor François Bouchardon, 1683
Oil on canvas, 111 × 89.5 cm

151

152

152
Hyacinthe Rigaud (1659–1743)
Portrait of Pierre Mignard, 1691
Oil on canvas, 140 × 111 cm

153
Hyacinthe Rigaud (1659–1743)
Portrait of the Artist, 1710–1711
Oil on canvas, 81 × 65 cm

154
The Hall of Battles, 1833–1837
Frédéric Nepveu (1777–1862) and Pierre-François-Léonard
Fontaine (1762–1853)

155
Eugène Delacroix (1798–1863)
The Battle of Taillebourg Won by Saint Louis
Oil on canvas, 485 × 555 cm, Drawing Room of 1837

156
Alexandre-Évariste Fragonard (1780–1850)
The Battle of Marignan, 1837
Oil on canvas, 465 × 543 cm

157
François Gérard (1770–1837)
Entry of Henry IV into Paris
Oil on canvas, 510 × 958 cm, Drawing Room of 1817

158

158
Léon Cogniet (1794–1880)
Portrait of Louis-Philippe d'Orléans, Duke of Chartres, in 1792, 1834
Oil on canvas, 135 × 95 cm, Drawing Room of 1792

159
Léon Cogniet (1794–1880)
*The Paris National Guard Assembled on the Pont Neuf
on Its Way to the Army, September 1792*
Oil on canvas, 189 × 204 cm, Drawing Room of 1792

160
South Ground Floor Stone Gallery
Frédéric Nepveu (1777–1862)

161
Jacques-Louis David (1748–1825)
The Tennis Court Oath, 1791
Fragment of an unfinished canvas
White chalk, heightened with wash of sanguine and black, oil on canvas, 370 × 654 cm

160

162

162
Antoine Jean Gros (1771–1835)
Portrait of the Artist, 1795
Oil on canvas, 49 × 40 cm

163
Anne-Louis Girodet de Roussy Trioson (1767–1824)
Portrait of the Artist, 1795
Oil on canvas, 49 × 40 cm

164
Antoine Jean Gros (1771–1835)
Bonaparte at the Bridge of Arcole, 1796
Oil on canvas, 130 × 94 cm

165
Jacques-Louis David (1748–1825)
Bonaparte Crossing the Alps
Oil on canvas, 271 × 232 cm

166
Anne-Louis Girodet de Roussy Trioson (1767–1824)
The Revolt of Cairo
Oil on canvas, 364 × 500 cm, Drawing Room of 1810

167
Anne-Louis Girodet de Roussy Trioson (1767–1824)
Portrait of Jean-Baptiste Belley, Deputy of Santo Domingo to Convention of France, 1797
Oil on canvas, 158 × 111 cm

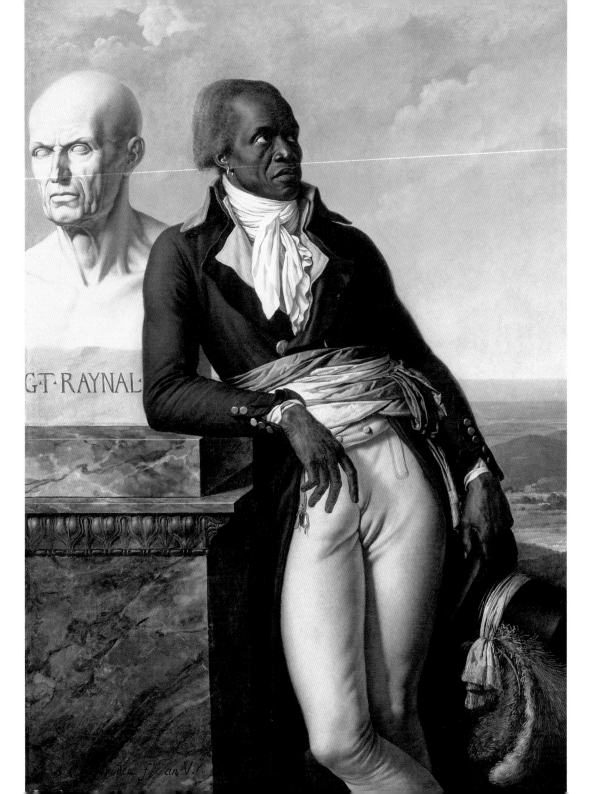

G·T·RAYNAL·

168
Antoine Jean Gros (1771–1835)
Napoleon Bonaparte Haranguing the Army Before the Battle of the Pyramids
Additions done in 1835–1836 by Auguste Debay
Oil on canvas, 389 × 311 cm, Drawing Room of 1810

169
Antoine Jean Gros (1771–1835)
The Battle of Abukir
Oil on canvas, 578 × 968 cm, Drawing Room of 1806

168

170

170
Andrea Appiani (1754–1817)
Portrait of the Comtesse Regnaud de Saint-Jean-d'Angély, ca. 1795
Oil on canvas, 70 × 55 cm

171
Élisabeth Vigée Lebrun (1755–1842)
*Portrait of Caroline Bonaparte, Queen of Naples,
with Her Daughter Laetitia Joséphine,* 1807
Oil on canvas, 217 × 143 cm

172

172
Robert Lefevre (1755–1830)
Portrait of François-Nicolas Mollien, Minister of the Public Treasury, 1806
Oil on canvas, 214 × 137 cm

173
Antoine Jean Gros (1771–1835)
Portrait of Comtesse Henriette Legrand
Oil on canvas, 245 × 172 cm, Drawing Room of 1812

174
Louis-François Lejeune (1775–1848)
Napoleon Visiting a Bivouac on the Eve of the Battle of Austerlitz
Oil on canvas, 180 × 220 cm, Drawing Room of 1808

175
Charles Meynier (1768–1832)
Marshal Ney and the Soldiers of the 76th Regiment
Retrieving their Flags on 7 November 1805
Oil on canvas, 360 × 524 cm, Drawing Room of 1808

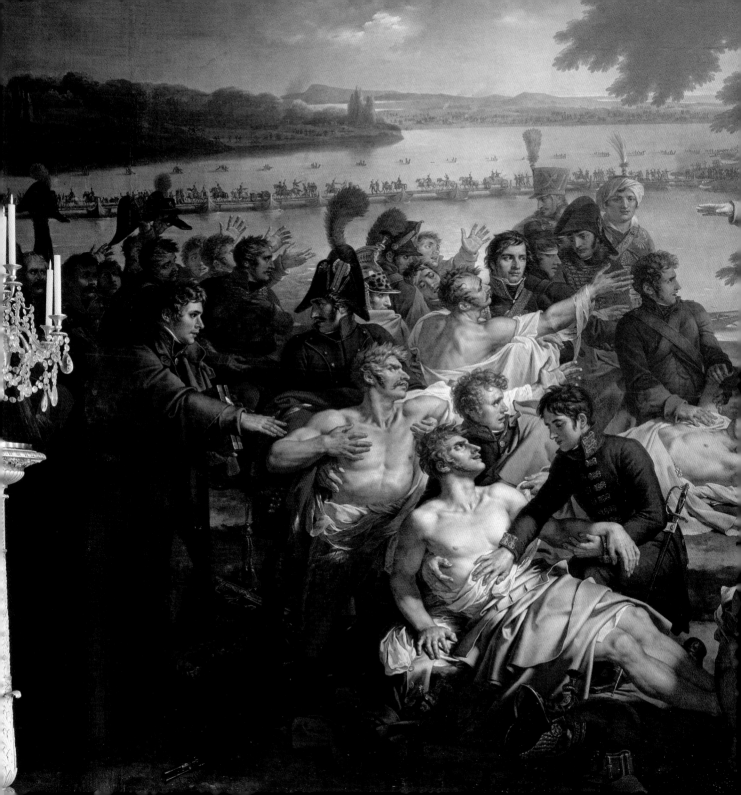

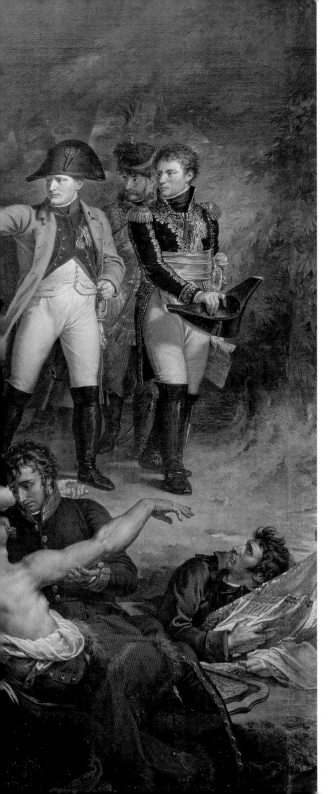

176
Charles Meynier (1768–1832)
Napoleon's Return to the Island of Lobau on the Danube
after the Battle of Essling
Oil on canvas, 473 × 529 cm

177
Louis-François Lejeune (1775–1848)
Assault on the Monastery of San Engracio in Zaragoza, 1827
Oil on canvas, 150 × 128 cm

178
Carle Vernet (1758–1836)
Napoleon at the Gates of Madrid Receiving a Deputation from the City, 3 December 1808
Addition by Éloi-Firmin Féron, 1834–1835
Oil on canvas, 361 × 500 cm, Drawing Room of 1810

PIVS · VII.   PONT· MAX·

180

179
Jacques-Louis David (1748–1825)
Portrait of Pope Pius VII
Oil on canvas, 91 × 85 cm

180
Robert Lefevre (1755–1830)
Portrait of Dominique Vivant Denon, 1808
Oil on canvas, 92 × 78 cm

181
Louis Ducis (1775–1847)
Portrait of Napoleon Bonaparte with His Nephews and Nieces on the Terrace at Saint-Cloud
Oil on canvas, 105 × 143 cm

182
Pietro Benvenuti (1769–1844)
Elisa Baciocchi, Grand Duchess of Tuscany, Surrounded by Her Court, 1813
Oil on canvas, 325 × 485 cm

183
Étienne–Barthélémy Garnier (1759–1849)
*The Entry of Napoleon and Marie-Louise into the Tuileries Gardens on
the Day of Their Wedding, 2 April 1810,* 1810
Oil on canvas, 327 × 495 cm

184
Eugène Isabey (1803–1886)
Loading the Ashes of Napoleon I Aboard the Belle
Poule *on October 15th, 1840,* 1842
Oil on canvas, 238 × 369 cm

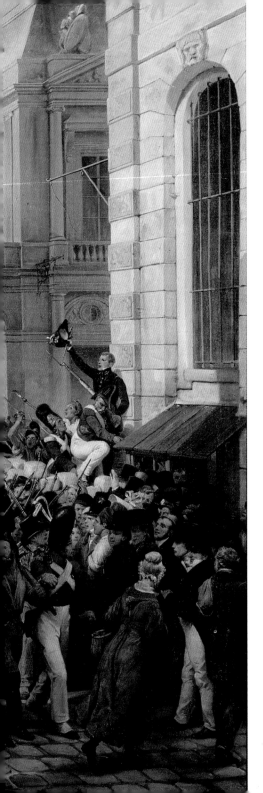

185
Horace Vernet (1789–1863)
*The Duke of Orleans Leaves the Palais-Royal and
Goes to the Hotel de Ville on 31st July 1830,* 1832
Oil on canvas, 215 × 261 cm, Drawing Room of 1833

186

186
Thomas Lawrence (1769–1830)
Portrait of François Gérard, 1824
Oil on wood panel, 70 × 58 cm

187
Franz-Xaver Winterhalter (1806–1873)
Louis-Philippe I, King of the French, 1841
Oil on canvas, 284 × 184 cm

188
Eugène Lami (1800–1890)
Fieschi's Assassination Attempt, July 28th, 1835, 1845
Oil on canvas, 57 × 277 cm

189
Théodore Chassériau (1819–1856)
Ali Ben Ahmed, the Last Caliph of Constantine, with His Entourage outside Constantine, 1845
Oil on canvas, 325 × 260 cm

190
Horace Vernet (1789–1863)
The Battle of Isly
Oil on canvas, 514 × 1040 cm

189

191
Horace Vernet (1789–1863)
The Battle of Habra, Algeria, December 1835, 1840
Oil on canvas, 512 × 713 cm

192
François-Auguste Biard (1798–1882)
*The Abolition of Slavery
in the French colonies in 1848*
Oil on canvas, 260 × 392 cm, Drawing Room of 1849

193
Louis Ambroise Garneray (1783–1857)
Naval Battle of Navarino, 1831
Oil on canvas, 179 × 277.8 cm

194
Franz-Xaver Winterhalter (1806–1873)
Portrait of Queen Victoria, 1842
Oil on canvas, 132 × 97 cm

195
Eugénie Servières (1784–1855)
*Ines de Castro with Her Children Throwing Herself
at the Feet of King Alfonso IV of Portugal,* 1822
Oil on canvas, 113 × 139 cm

196

196
François Gérard (1770–1837)
Portrait of Alphonse de Lamartine, 1831
Oil on canvas, 118 × 91 cm

197
Hippolyte Flandrin (1809–1864)
Napoleon III in His Grand Cabinet at the Tuileries, 1862
Oil on canvas, 212 × 147 cm

198

199

198
Théodore Chassériau (1819–1856)
Portrait of Alexis de Tocqueville, 1850
Oil on canvas, 163 × 130 cm

199
Johann Olaf Södermark,
Portrait of Henri Beyle, Called Stendhal, 1840
Oil on canvas, 62 × 50 cm

200
Adolphe Yvon (1817–1893)
Sketch or copy of *The Capture of the Malakoff Tower*
By General Mac-Mahon, on September 8th, 1855, 1857
Oil on canvas, 71.5 × 108 cm

201
Édouard Dubufe (1819–1883)
Portrait of Eugénie de Montijo, Empress of the French, 1854
Oil on canvas, 138 × 98 cm

202
Jean Léon Gérôme (1824–1904)
The Reception of the Siamese Ambassadors at Fontainebleau by Napoleon III and the Empress Eugénie
in the Ballroom of the Palace of Fontainebleau, on June 27th, 1861, 1864
Oil on canvas, 120 × 260 cm

203
Théobald Chartran (1849–1907)
The Ceremony at the Pantheon to Celebrate the Centenary of the Birth of Victor Hugo,
on February 26th, 1902, in the Presence of President Félix Loubet, 1904
Oil on canvas, 225 × 182 cm

204

204
Gustave Courbet (1819–1877)
Portrait of Henri Rochefort, ca. 1873–1874
Oil on canvas, 65 × 54 cm

205
André Devambez (1867–1944)
The Barricade, 1871
Oil on canvas, 140 × 107 cm

206
Jean-François Raffaelli (1850–1924)
Georges Clemenceau Giving a Speech at the Cirque Fernando, 1883
Oil on canvas, 243 × 205 cm

GEORGES LEROUX

207
Georges Paul Leroux (1877–1957)
Les Éparges: Soldiers Burying Their Comrades by Moonlight
Oil on canvas, 183 × 262 cm

THE GARDENS
AND THE PARK

THE GARDENS AND THE PARK

The first description of Versailles by Madeleine de Scudéry concerns the gardens only: In 1669, in *La Promenade de Versailles*, the author writes of a pretty foreigner discovering the setting of the first festivities and the fountains. Twenty years later, in *La Manière de montrer les jardins* (*The Way to Show the Gardens*), Louis XIV describes the gigantic projects of André Le Nôtre, who created a French-style garden punctuated with parterres, statues, basins, and fountains. Water is the favored ornament of the gardens, and there are many magnificent vantage points from which visitors can appreciate the impressive waterworks, channeled by a powerful pump to the reservoirs and basins.

Today, as in the past, the park is a spectacle dominated by perspective and symmetry, and it can best be appreciated from the central axis, which runs perpendicular to the château. The *Parterre d'eau* (Water Parterre), which is made up of two larger rectangular pools, extends from the base of the Hall of Mirrors and flows into the Latona Basin and its pyramidal fountain. The twenty-four statues decorating the *Parterre d'Eau* were part of the great commission of 1674, created under the supervision

of Charles Le Brun. The vegetation is treated as ornamentation in much the same way as the sculpture. The gaze then descends the *Allée Royale* (Royal Walk) all the way to the Basin of Apollo, which serves as an introduction to the Grand Canal. An impetuous four-horse chariot emerges from the water, *Apollo in His Chariot*, a sculpture by Tuby based on a drawing by Charles Le Brun. The Grand Canal, which began excavation in 1668, was used during the reign of Louis XIV for naval demonstrations and battles: Fifteen gondolas sent by the Venetian Republic were used in processions and festivities.

On either side of the opening of the *Allée Royale* (also known as the *Tapis Vert*, literally the "green carpet") paths lead into the groves or small rooms of greenery embellished with fountains and statues. These groves make up what remains of the grand estate that was once dedicated to hunting. On the north side, the path descends toward the Fountain of Neptune, enlivened with spouting water, by way of the Avenue of the Marmosets, the Fountain of the Pyramid, the Grove of the Arch of Triumph, and the Fountain of the Dragon. There are a seemingly unending number of places to explore, from the

Bosquets du Midi, or South Groves, which alternate shadow and light, to the somber rococo steps of the open-air Ball Room, to the gleaming white stone of the Colonnade built by Jules Hardouin-Mansart.

The construction of the gardens and groves were as constant as the decoration and construction of the palace. At the end of the Ancien Régime, the paths were opened to the public to a greater extent, while Louis XVI ordered the removal of centuries-old trees. In 1776, Hubert Robert designed the grove and the Baths of Apollo. This English-style garden supplanted the French style; groves and greenery were favored over excessively costly fountains. But the parterres throughout the palace's grounds continued to arouse the admiration of the many visitors, even after the French Revolution, including Alfred de Musset and Théophile Gautier, as well as Anna de Noailles and Marcel Proust.

Although the gardens of Versailles were designed for parties, they are also educational and functional spaces. Sculptures that illustrate fables and mythology are plentiful, while the land and buildings provide opportunities to engage in scientific experimentation. The *Pièce d'Eau des Suisses* (Lake of the Swiss Guard) has been used for training the French Navy. Nearby, Jean de La Quintinie installed a vegetable garden and an orchard as early as 1679, which provided fruit and vegetables for the king's table. The Orangerie, a greenhouse, flanked by the *Cent-Marches*, or the Stair of One Hundred Steps, located near the *Parterre du Midi*, or South Parterre, is a source of fruit. During winter, the interior of the Orangerie is a dark and heavily scented forest where narrow paths make it possible to wander freely. In summer, myrtle plants, oleanders, lemon trees, and orange trees adorn the parterres. Also in summer, when the trees that have spent the winter inside are moved out to the parterre, it is possible to get a sense of the majesty of the immense gallery within the Orangerie: Built between 1681 and 1688 by Jules Hardouin-Mansart, it is more than 490 feet (150 meters) long and crowned by a barrel vault—truly a masterpiece of stonecutting.

208
Main Facade of the Exterior Structure, or the "New Palace"
Jules Hardouin-Mansart (1646–1708)

209
Jean Raon (1631–1707) and Corneille Van Cleve (1644–1735)
Battle Between a Lion and a Prone Wolf, 1685–1687
Bronze, 137 × 226 × 118 cm

210
Thomas Regnaudin (1622–1706)
The Loire Valley, 1686–1689
Bronze, 135 × 243 × 104 cm, Water Parterre

211
Western Facade of the Palace and the North Wing from the Water Parterre
Jules Hardouin-Mansart (1646–1708)

212
The Water Parterre and the Grand Canal Seen
from the Balcony of the Hall of Mirrors
André Le Nôtre (1613–1700)

213
Jean-Baptiste Tuby (1635–1700)
Vase of Peace, 1684–1685
Marble, Terrace of the Water Parterre and the Western Facade of the Palace

214
The Royal Alley
André le Nôtre (1613–1700) and Jules Hardouin-Mansart (1646–1708)
The Basin of Latona, 1668–1686
Gaspard (1629–1681) and Balthasar (1628–1674) Marsy
Lead, bronze, and stone

344

215
The Basin of Latona from the Royal Alley or Green Carpet
Gaspard (1629–1681) and Balthasar (1628–1674) Marsy

216
L. Lecomte, after Pierre Mignard (1612–1695)
Hercules, 1684–1686
Marble, 285 × 118 × 88 cm
Jean Dedieu (1646–1727), **after Pierre Mignard** (1612–1695)
Bacchante, 1684–1685
Marble, 280 × 93 × 67 cm, Parterre of Latona

217
Auguste Edme Suchelet (1854–1932), after Antoine Coysevox (1683–1685)
Nymph with a Seashell, 1890–1891
Marble, 110 × 191 × 82 cm, Parterre of Latona

218
Georges Sibrayque (before 1652–1682) and Jean Cornu (1650–1710),
after Gaspard Marsy (1629–1681) and Charles Le Brun (1619–1690)
Africa, 1675–1682
Marble, North Parterre

219
After Benoît Massou
The Earth
Concrete mixed with powdered marble, 240 × 120 × 84 cm, North Parterre

220
After Pierre Mazeline
Europe
Cast, 246 × 96 × 79 cm, North Parterre

221
Noël Jouvenet (?–1716), after Charles Le Brun (1619–1690)
Le Sanguin, 1675–1680
Marble, 235 × 101 × 92 cm, North Parterre

222
The Basin of Apollo, 1668–1670
Jean-Baptiste Tuby (1635–1700)
Gilt lead

223
The Royal Alley or the *Tapis Vert* and
the Western Facade of the Palace
In the foreground, The Basin of Apollo, 1668–1670
Jean-Baptiste Tuby (1635–1700)

222

224

224 | 225
The Basin of Apollo, 1668–1670
Jean-Baptiste Tuby (1635–1700)
Gilt lead

226
The Basin of Apollo

227
Walkway to the Basin of Apollo

228
The Western Facade of the Palace and the Royal Alley
or the *Tapis Vert*, from the Grand Canal

229
The South Parterre and the Swiss Lake

230
The Orangerie
Jules Hardouin-Mansart (1646–1708)
The Parterre of the Orangerie
André Le Nôtre (1613–1700)

231
The Orangerie
Jules Hardouin-Mansart (1646–1708)
The Parterre of the Orangerie
André Le Nôtre (1613–1700)

232
The Parterre of the Orangerie
André Le Nôtre (1613–1700)

233
The Stair of One Hundred Steps

234

234 | 235
The Grove of the Rock Garden or Ballroom, 1680–1683

236
Basin of the Girandole

237
Apollo Pothos
Marble, Basin of the Water Mirror

239

238 | 239
The King's Garden
South Groves

240
Hall of the Chestnut Trees, 1704

241
The Colonnade, 1685
Jules Hardouin-Mansart (1646–1708), Marble
At the center: After François Bouchardon (1677–1699)
The Rape of Proserpine, 1990

242
The Colonnade, 1685
Jules Hardouin-Mansart (1646–1708)
Marble

243
The North Parterre

245

244
The Water Parterre

245
L. Lecomte, after Pierre Mignard (1612–1695)
Hercules, 1684–1686
Marble, 285 × 118 × 88 cm, Parterre of Latona
Jean Dedieu (1646–1727), after Pierre Mignard (1612–1695)
Bacchante, 1684–1685
Marble, 280 × 93 × 67 cm, Parterre of Latona

246
The Basin of the Pyramid, 1679
François Girardon (1628–1715), after Charles Le Brun (1619–1690)
North Parterre and North Wing

247

247
François Girardon (1628–1715)
The Bath of the Nymphs of Diana, 1668–1670
Lead, 132 × 605 × 25.5 cm, Water Alley, called the *Allée des Marmousets*

248
François Girardon (1628–1715)
The Bath of the Nymphs of Diana, 1679
Detail

249

249
Jacques Buirette (1631–1699)
Group of Children Supporting a Basin
Bronze, 146 × 109 cm, Water Alley, called the *Allée des Marmousets*

250
The Water Alley, Called the *Allée des Marmousets*
Claude Perrault (1613–1688)
North Parterre

251
The Dragon Basin
Detail

252
The Dragon Basin and the Water Alley,
Called the *Allée des Marmousets*

253
The Neptune Basin, 1679–1681
André Le Nôtre (1613–1700)

255

254
Domenico Guidi
Fame Writing the History of the King, 1677–1686
Marble, Neptune Basin

255
Jean-Baptiste Tuby (1635–1700), Antoine Coysevox (1640–1720),
and Jacques Prou (1655–1706)
The Fountain of France Triumphant, 1679–1683
Gilt lead, Grove of the Arch of Triumph

256

256 | 257
The Grove of the Three Fountains, 1677
André Le Nôtre (1613–1700)

258

258
François Girardon (1628–1715)
Apollo Served by the Nymphs, 1664–1672
Marble

259
The Grove of the Baths of Apollo, 1778
Hubert Robert (1733–1808)

260
The Grove of Domes, 1675–1677
Jules Hardouin-Mansart (1646–1708) and André Le Nôtre (1613–1700)
Basin, François Girardon (1628–1715),
Marble

261
The Grove of Enceladus
Gaspard Marsy (1629–1681)
Fountain of Enceladus, 1675–1677
Gilt lead

260

262
The Fountain of Enceladus, 1675–1677
Gaspard Marsy (1629–1681)
Gilt lead

263
The Fountain of the Obelisk, 1704
Jules Hardouin-Mansart (1646–1708)

264

264
The Basin of Bacchus, or of Autumn, 1672–1675
Gaspard Marsy (1629–1681), after Charles Le Brun (1619–1690)
Gilt lead and paint

265
The Basin of Ceres, or of Summer
Thomas Regnaudin (1622–1706), after Charles Le Brun (1619–1690)
Lead, 147 × 335 × 336 cm

266
The Basin of Saturn, or of Winter
François Girardon (1628–1715), after Charles Le Brun (1619–1690)
Gilt lead, 140 × 350 × 350 cm

267
The Basin of Flora, or of Spring
Jean-Baptiste Tuby (1635–1700), after Charles Le Brun (1619–1690)
Lead, 155 × 355 × 350 cm

THE CHÂTEAUX OF TRIANON

THE CHÂTEAUX OF TRIANON

In 1670, on the land of the old village of Trianon to the north of the Grand Canal, Louis Le Vau began construction on the Porcelain Trianon, topping it with a Chinese-style roof. The outer walls are decorated with faience tiles in white-and-blue motifs. The fragility of this material hastened its dilapidation. Jules Hardouin-Mansart built the Grand Trianon as early as 1687, described by Saint-Simon as "a small palace of marble and porphyry with a delightful garden." This residence gave the French kings a place to withdraw from court life, but was also the setting for sumptuous fetes.

Across from the entrance, visitors encounter a colonnade that links the two wings. The facades are punctuated by pink marble pillars. Topping the structure is a flat, Italian-style roof concealed behind a balustrade. A single-story building, the Grand Trianon adjoins the parterres constructed by André Le Nôtre. During the reign of Louis XIV, the flowers were changed every day.

Only the royal family was allowed to enter this palace, where the serving staff was reduced to the bare minimum. Louis XIV spent brief periods of time here. The *Salon Frais*, or Cool Drawing Room, the *Salon des Sources*, or Drawing Room of the Springs, and the gallery still feature wood carvings executed at the king's behest during the very last years of his reign. In the middle of the eighteenth century, Louis XV renovated his apartment to suit his tastes. By this point, the palace featured a reception room, a dining room, and a drawing room for company.

After the French Revolution, Napoleon kept a suite of apartments at the Trianon with Marie Louise. He refurnished the palace and ordered improvements for the surrounding grounds. The Emperor's Small Apartment, with the Drawing Room of the Malachites, is a mark of his stay. Louis Philippe later renovated some of the rooms.

In 1763, Louis XV ordered the construction of a relatively unadorned pavilion with a square floor plan to the northwest of the Grand Trianon for Madame de Pompadour, although she died before construction was completed. This was the Petit Trianon, built by Ange-Jacques Gabriel *à la grecque*, or in the new Greek revival style. With the five windows of its facade, the building displays as much nobility as sobriety. Louis XV frequently spent time there in the company of Madame du Barry. An impassioned botanist and amateur of the natural sciences, the king ordered the construction of a menagerie for domestic animals, hothouses, a number of pleasure pavilions, a French-style garden, and a botanical garden (neither of which outlasted the vogue for the picturesque Anglo-Chinese garden).

From the very beginning of his reign, Louis XVI in effect handed over the keys of the Petit Trianon to Marie Antoinette. The building soon became the private domain of the queen, who appointed the architect Richard Mique to renovate it. Upstairs, one progresses from the antechamber to the large dining room, then to the small dining room, and from there to the drawing room for visitors. This is the queen's apartment. Nothing is rigid or stiff: The wainscotings are adorned with flowers sculpted from nature, with trophies, and with the monogram of the king. Lilies were no longer the emblems of royalty, but a garden theme was imposed on the interior decoration. The decorated lintels, whose themes were taken from Ovid's *Metamorphoses*, paid homage to the flowers. The mezzanine was also reserved for the queen, while the attic housed the king's apartment.

Eugénie, the niece of Marie Antoinette, began the restoration of this building. Transformed into a hotel during the French Revolution, the Petit Trianon was used during the Empire by Pauline Borghese. Later, during the July Monarchy, it was used by the Duke of Orléans.

Marie Antoinette destroyed the greenhouses and the gardens, but she preserved the buildings erected by Louis XV, the *Pavillon Français* (French Pavilion) and the *Salon Frais* (Cool Drawing Room). She added the Temple of Love and, most notably, the theater, which only the royal family was permitted to attend. Most important, she had Richard Mique build a hamlet of a dozen or so rustic buildings. This full-fledged working farm was dominated by the *Maison de la Reine*, or Queen's House, recognizable by its gallery.

268
The Grand Trianon and the Parterres, 1687
Jules Hardouin-Mansart (1646–1708)
and André Le Nôtre (1613–1700)

269
Colonnade or Peristyle of the Grand Trianon, 1687
Jules Hardouin-Mansart (1646–1708)
and Robert de Cotte (1656–1735)
Marble

270
The Grand Trianon Seen from the Parterres, 1687
Jules Hardouin-Mansart (1646–1708) and André Le Nôtre (1613–1700)

271
The Grand Trianon Seen from the Parterres, 1687
Jules Hardouin-Mansart (1646–1708) and André Le Nôtre (1613–1700)

272

27

272
The Drawing Room of Mirrors or
Grand Cabinet of the Empress
Letter-box Desk or Money-box Desk, First Empire
François Honoré Jacob-Desmalter (1770–1841)
Mahogany

273
The Empress's Bedchamber

275

274
Door- and Windowframes of the Round Drawing Room
Jules Hardouin-Mansart (1646–1708) and Ange-Jacques Gabriel (1698–1782)

275
Family Drawing Room, 1838
Family Table, 1837,
George-Alphonse Jacob-Desmalter (1799–1870)

276
Malachite Drawing Room
Malachite Basin, Russia, 1807, on a tripod,
after Pierre Cartellier (1757–1831)
Malachite Pedestal Table, assembled by Charles Percier (1764–1838)

277
Charles de La Fosse (1636–1716)
Clytia Changed into a Sunflower, 1678
Oil on canvas, overdoor of the Malachite Drawing Room

278
The Cool Drawing Room, or *Salon Frais*, or Large Cabinet of the Emperor
Jean-Baptiste Martin (1659–1735)
Left: *View of the Palace of Versailles from the Dragon Basin and the Neptune Basin*
Right: *View of the Town and the Palace of Versailles from the Hill of Montbauron*
Oil on canvas, 260 × 184 cm

279
Cotelle Gallery
Jules Hardouin-Mansart (1646–1708)

280
Jean Cotelle (1645–1708)
View of the Parterres of Trianon with Flora and Zephyr
Oil on canvas, 210 × 139 cm, Cotelle Gallery

281
Bedchamber of the Emperor
Boiserie from the era of Louis XV

283

283
Louis de Boullogne
Apollo and the Sybil
Oil on canvas, 110 × 90 cm

284
Buffet d'Eau, 1702–1703
After Jules Hardouin-Mansart (1646–1708)
Garden of the Grand Trianon

285
Petit Trianon, 1761–1768
Ange-Jacques Gabriel (1698–1782)
Parterres
Claude and Antoine Richard

286
Grand Staircase of the Petit Trianon, 1768
Ange-Jacques Gabriel (1698–1782)
Flight with the Monogram of Marie Antoinette, François Brochois

287
Élisabeth Vigée Lebrun (1755–1842)
Portrait of Marie Antoinette with a Rose, 1783
Oil on canvas, 113 × 87 cm

288
Company Drawing Room
Pedestal Table, Bernard Molitor (1755–1833)
Piano, 1790, Pascal Taskin (1723–1793)
Music Stand, 1779, Gilles-Pierre Cauvet (1731–1788)
Lantern, 1785, Pierre-Philippe Thomire (1751–1843)
Boiserie from the era of Louis XV

289
The Bedroom of Marie Antoinette
Georges Jacob (1739–1814)
Ear-of-Wheat Furniture, 1787, walnut carved by
Pierre-Claude Triquet and Jean-Baptiste Simon Rode and
painted in natural style by Jean-Baptiste Chaillot de Prusse

290
The Theater of the Queen, 1778–1780
Richard Mique (1728–1794)
Groups of sculptures on the proscenium, torchères and groups of children in the arches
Joseph Deschamps
Pasteboard
On the stage, the set decoration for *La Forêt*, performed in 1835
Pierre-Luc Cicéri

291
The French Pavilion at Trianon, 1749–1750
Ange-Jacques Gabriel (1698–1782)

292

292
The Rock, after Hubert Robert (1733–1808)
The Belvedere at the Petit Trianon, 1778–1781, Richard Mique (1728–1794)
Exterior Decoration, Joseph Deschamps

293
The Belvedere at the Petit Trianon, 1778–1781
Richard Mique (1728–1794)
Louis Mansiaux, called Chevalier
Painted Stucco by Sébastien-François Leriche

294
The Temple of Love, 1777
Richard Mique (1728–1794)
Cupid Cutting His Bow from the Club of Hercules (1750), 1778,
Louis-Philippe Mouchy, after Edme Bouchardon
Marble

295
The Farm of the Hamlet with the Marlborough Tower,
the House of the Queen at Trianon, and the Large Lake, 1783
Richard Mique (1728–1794)

294

296

296
The House of the Queen at Trianon, 1783
Richard Mique (1728–1794)

297
The Mill of the Hamlet of the Queen at Trianon, 1783
Richard Mique (1728–1794)

29

INDEX

CREDITS

The publisher would like to thank:
Jean-Baptiste Leroux for his time and his involvement in
this project, and
Caroline de Lambertye and Stéphane Brochier at RMN.

Public institution of the Palace, the Museum, and the
National Estate of Versailles
Jean-Vincent Bacquart, director of publications, with
the assistance of Émilie Jacques

Editorial director: Brigitte Govignon
Graphic design: Noémie Levain

Abrams edition
Editor: Laura Dozier
Design: Shawn Dahl, dahlimama inc
Production Mananger: Jules Thomson

Cataloging-in-Publication Data has been applied for and
may be obtained from the Library of Congress.
ISBN: 978-1-4197-0067-5
Museum edition ISBN: 978-1-4197-0353-9

Printed and bound in China
10 9 8 7 6 5 4 3 2 1

Abrams books are available at special discounts when
purchased in quantity for premiums and promotions as
well as fundraising or educational use. Special editions
can also be created to specification. For details, contact
specialsales@abramsbooks.com or the address below.

115 West 18th Street
New York, NY 10011
www.abramsbooks.com